Colour-Coding & Maps

Each chapter has a colour code along the banner at the top of the page that is also used for text and symbols on maps (eg all venues reviewed in the Highlights chapter are orange on the maps). The fold-out maps inside the front and back covers are numbered from 1 to 6. All sights and venues in the text have map references; eg (3, B3) means Map 3, grid reference B3. See p96 for map symbols.

Prices

Multiple prices listed with reviews (eg 600/300Ft) usually indicate adult/concession admission to a venue. Concession prices can include senior, student, member or coupon discounts. Meal cost and room rate categories are listed at the start of the Eating and Sleeping chapters, respectively.

Text Symbols

- ☎ telephone
- ✉ address
- 🖳 email/website address
- € admission
- ☺ opening hours
- ⓘ information
- Ⓜ metro
- 🚍 bus
- 🚋 tram
- 🚎 trolleybus
- 🚆 train
- ⚓ ferry
- ✖ on-site/nearby eatery

Best of Budapest
1st edition – January 2007

Published by Lonely Planet Publications Pty Ltd
ABN 36 005 607 983

Australia Head Office, Locked Bag 1, Footscray, Vic 3011
  ☎ 03 8379 8000 fax 03 8379 8111
  🖳 talk2us@lonelyplanet.com.au
USA 150 Linden St, Oakland, CA 94607
  ☎ 510 893 8555 toll free 800 275 8555
  fax 510 893 8572
  🖳 info@lonelyplanet.com
UK 72–82 Rosebery Avenue, London EC1R 4RW
  ☎ 020 7841 9000 fax 020 7841 9001
  🖳 go@lonelyplanet.co.uk

This title was commissioned in Lonely Planet's London office by Janine Eberle and produced by Cambridge Publishing Management Limited. **Thanks** to David Connolly, Jackie Dobbyne, Tony Fankhauser, Quentin Frayne, Mark Germanchis, Mark Griffiths, Laura Jane, Valentina Kremenchutskaya, Amanda Learmonth, Kate McDonald, Tim Newton, Malisa Plesa, Glenn van der Knijff

Photographs by Lonely Planet Images and Richard Nebesky except for the following: p5, p6, p10, p20, p26, p28, p57, p77 David Greedy/Lonely Planet Images; p8, p21, p36, p46 Martin Moos/Lonely Planet Images; p9, p13 Kim Grant/Lonely Planet Images; p14, p30, p31, p32, p80 Jonathan Smith/Lonely Planet Images ; p37 Roberto Soncin Gerometta/Lonely Planet Images; p66 Guy Moberly/Lonely Planet Images; p7, p17, p24, p29, p35, p67 Rafael Estefania; p16 Vick Fisher/Alamy; p19 Oliver Benn/Alamy.

Cover photograph Gypsy street musicians in Budapest, Paul Bernhardt/Lonely Planet Images.

All images are copyright of the photographers unless otherwise indicated. Many of the images in this guide are available for licensing from Lonely Planet Images: www .lonelyplanetimages.com.

ISBN 9 781 74179 121 1

Printed through Colorcraft Ltd, Hong Kong.
Printed in China

Contents

From the Publisher

THE AUTHOR
Steve Fallon

Steve made his first visit to Budapest during the early 1980s with three things on his 'to do' list: (1) visit a thermal spa; (2) drink masses of Tokaj wine; and (3) buy some fruit for his friends in Poland whose children, born under the neofascist regime of General Wojciech Jaruzelski, had never seen (much less tasted) such 'exotics' as bananas. Having accomplished all three, he visited Budapest again and again, moving there in 1992, where he learned to love the Hungarian language, *pálinka* and very hot thermal water – not necessarily in that order. Now based in London, Steve returns to Budapest regularly for a fix of all three. He has worked on every edition of Lonely Planet's *Budapest* and *Hungary* guides.

In Budapest, thanks to Bea Szirti for all her helpful suggestions and to Erzsébet Tiszai, who assisted with the research. Brandon Krueger of the Central European University and Eric D'Amato of Pestiside.hu added insights into what's on in Budapest after dark. Ildikó Nagy Moran, also at the Central European University, was as always welcoming, helpful and generous. In London, thanks to commissioning editor Janine Eberle, who made it all possible. As is the custom, I dedicate these efforts to my Partner – capital 'p' at long last – Michael Rothschild, with love and gratitude and lots and lots of Budapest memories.

LONELY PLANET AUTHORS
Why is our travel information the best in the world? It's simple: our authors are independent, dedicated travellers. They don't research using just the internet or phone, and they don't take freebies in exchange for positive coverage. They travel widely, to all the popular spots and off the beaten track. They personally visit thousands of hotels, restaurants, cafés, bars, galleries, palaces, museums and more – and they take pride in getting all the details right, and telling it how it is. For more, see the authors' section on **www.lonelyplanet.com.**

PHOTOGRAPHER
Richard Nebesky

Richard was born one snowy night in the grungy Prague suburb of Zizkov, but surprisingly he didn't have a camera in his hand. It was, however, not long after he got out of his cot that his father, an avid photo enthusiast, gave him his first point-and-shoot unit. Ever since, the camera has been by his side on wander treks, ski adventures and cycling trips, and while researching Lonely Planet books around the globe. He has also worked for various magazines and travel guide publishers and on many social photography projects.

Photographing Budapest in winter, with regular drizzle and grey skies, was a challenge. Just as well that this imperial city of the former Hungarian empire is full of such wonderfully photogenic structures.

SEND US YOUR FEEDBACK
We love to hear from travellers – your comments keep us on our toes and help make our books better. Our well-travelled team reads every word on what you loved or loathed about this book. Although we cannot reply individually to postal submissions, we always guarantee that your feedback goes straight to the appropriate authors, in time for the next edition – and the most useful submissions are rewarded with a free book. To send us your updates – and find out about Lonely Planet events, newsletters and travel news – visit our award-winning website: **www.lonelyplanet.com/feedback.**

Note: We may edit, reproduce and incorporate your comments in Lonely Planet products such as guidebooks, websites and digital products, so let us know if you don't want your comments reproduced or your name acknowledged. For a copy of our privacy policy, visit **www.lonelyplanet.com/privacy.**

Introducing Budapest

Budapest has all but exhausted the number of superlatives that can reasonably be applied to any world-class city. Not surprisingly, though, most of them still apply. It's the physical beauty of Budapest – both divinely created and manmade – that sets it apart from other cities of Eastern and Central Europe. Straddling a gentle curve in the Danube River, Budapest is flanked by the Buda Hills on its west bank and what is essentially the start of the Great Plain to the east. Architecturally, it is a gem, with enough baroque, neoclassical and Art Nouveau architecture to satisfy anyone.

Grander than Prague and more cosmopolitan than Warsaw, Budapest was for more than half a century (1867–1918) the joint imperial capital of the Austro-Hungarian empire. Accordingly it has a fin-de-siècle feel, for it was then, during the industrial boom and Budapest's 'golden age', that most of what you see today was built. As a result, it looks like a real, workaday city – with ring roads and trams and large leafy parks – and not a film set, overrun by gawpers.

With parks brimming with attractions, museums filled with treasures, pleasure boats sailing up and down the scenic Danube Bend, Turkish-era thermal baths belching steam and a nightlife throbbing until dawn most nights, the Hungarian capital is one of the Continent's most delightful and fun cities.

Men playing chess in the warm waters of the Széchenyi Baths

Neighbourhoods

Budapest is a large, sprawling city measuring 525 sq km. Its borders are Csepel Island in the Danube River to the south, the start of the Danube Bend to the north, westernmost Buda and the Buda Hills to the west and easternmost Pest and the start of the Great Plain to the east. The city is divided into 23 *kerület*, or districts, which have both numbers and traditional names, such as Újlipótváros (New Leopold Town) in district XIII or Víziváros (Watertown) in district I. The Roman numeral appearing before each street address signifies the district.

OFF THE BEATEN TRACK

You can beat the crowds and the beaten track by heading for any of the following lesser-known attractions:
- Gül Baba's Tomb (p24)
- The Japanese Garden (Margaret Island; p14)
- Kerepes Cemetery (p28)
- The Kiscelli Museum & Municipal Gallery (p21)
- The Roman Civilian Amphitheatre (Aquincum; p19)

Two ring roads – the Nagykörút (literally the 'Big Ring Road') and the semicircular Kiskörút (the 'Little Ring Road') – more or less link all of the most important bridges crossing the Danube and define central Pest. Within the confines of the Little Ring Road, you'll find the Inner Town (Belváros), the heart of Pest with posh Váci utca and central Vörösmarty tér, and the Northern Inner Town (or Lipótváros), with its commercial offices and government buildings. Outside these borders but within the Big Ring Road are – clockwise from north – leafy, very 'uptown' Újlipótváros; Terézváros, named in honour of Empress Maria Theresa; Erzsébetváros, containing much of what you'll want to see and eat and drink and buy in Pest; and the workaday districts of Józsefváros and Ferencváros.

Buda is dominated by Castle and Gellért Hills; the main square on this side is Moszkva tér. North from here are the districts of the Tabán, Víziváros, ancient Óbuda and even older Aquincum, site of the first Roman settlement.

Lying between the two, but neither Buda nor Pest, is teardrop-shaped Margaret Island, the city's lung and playground.

Gül Baba, an Ottoman dervish and poet, whose tomb may be visited (p24)

Itineraries

Budapest is chock-a-block with things to see and do. If you want a general overview of Budapest before striking out on your own, take one of the organised tours described in the Trips & Tours chapter (p37).

Day One

Spend most of the day on **Castle Hill** (p8), taking in the views and the sights, and visiting a museum or two. In the afternoon, ride the **Sikló** (p9) down to Clark Ádám tér and, depending on the day of the week, make your way to the **Király** or the **Gellért Baths** (p10) for a relaxing soak. In the evening, head for Liszt Ferenc tér for drinks and dinner at **Menza** (p53).

Day Two

Concentrate first on the two icons of Hungarian nationhood: the Crown of St Stephen in **Parliament** (p12) and the saint-king's mortal remains in the **Basilica of St Stephen** (p13). Take a late afternoon coffee (and cake) break at **Gerbeaud** (p61) in Vörösmarty tér, and get to the **Hungarian State Opera House** (p67) before going clubbing.

Day Three

Take one of the walking tours described in the Trips & Tours chapter, such as the one up **Andrássy út** (p33). The café **Lukács** (p61) is conveniently located en route, and you could even take the waters at the **Széchenyi Baths** (p10) in the City Park. **Robinson** (p56) is a convenient place for an evening meal. Then take a well-watered tour of the city's best 'gardens' (see p60).

WORST OF BUDAPEST

- *Konzumlányok* – the 'consume girls' in collusion with rip-off bars and clubs who take gullible guys for a ride
- Incessant road works – won't Budapest look great when it's done?
- *Csak magayarul* – the Magyar inability (or unwillingness) to speak foreign languages
- Meeting meat – anyone for that favourite Hungarian dish 'meat-stuffed meat'?
- *Honfibú* – the 'patriotic sorrow' trait that can make people here such downers (see p79) and raises the suicide rate

The impressive Parliament building, as seen from Castle Hill

Highlights

CASTLE HILL (4, B4)

Castle Hill (Várhegy), a 1km-long limestone plateau towering 170m above the Danube, contains Budapest's most important medieval monuments and museums, and is a Unesco World Heritage Site. It is the premier sight in the capital, and with its grand views and so many things to see, you should start your visit to the city here.

The walled area consists of two distinct parts: the **Old Town**, where commoners lived in the Middle Ages, and the **Royal Palace**, the original site of the castle built by King Béla IV in the 13th century.

INFORMATION

✉ I Várhegy
Ⓜ M2 Moszkva tér, then Várbusz
✖ Café Pierott (p47)

The best way to see the Old Town is to stroll (see p31) along the four medieval streets that more or less run parallel to one another and converge on Szentháromság tér, poking your head into the attractive little courtyards and visiting the odd museum.

A brief tour of the Old Town in one of the horse-drawn hackney cabs *(fiáker)* standing in Szentháromság tér will cost from 2000Ft per person. Or you might want to get the lie of the land by climbing to the top of the **Vienna Gate** (Bécsi kapu), rebuilt in 1936 at the northern end of the Old Town to mark the 250th anniversary of the retaking of the castle from the Turks. The centre of the district is **Szentháromság tér**, in the middle of which is a monumental **statue of the Holy Trinity**, one of the 'plague pillars' put up by grateful Buda citizens in the early 18th century. The square is dominated by Castle Hill's two most famous sights. The first is **Matthias Church** (☎ 355 5657; www. matyas-templom.hu; I Szentháromság tér 2; € 600/400Ft, family 1000Ft; ☻ 9am-5pm Mon-Fri, 9am-1pm Sat, 1-5pm Sun), a neo-Gothic creation with a colourful tiled roof designed by the architect Frigyes Schulek in 1896. It also has remarkable stained-glass windows, frescoes and wall decorations by the Romantic painters Károly Lotz and Bertalan Székely.

The stunning interior of Matthias Church

Just east of the church is the iconic **Fishermen's Bastion** (€ 330/165Ft; ☉ 9am-11pm), a neo-Gothic masquerade built as a viewing platform in 1905, and still offering among the best views in Budapest.

The Royal Palace section of Castle Hill is teeming with important monuments and museums, and on no account should you miss visiting the **Hungarian National Gallery** (p22) or the **Budapest History Museum** (p20).

DON'T MISS
- The collection of ecclesiastical art in Matthias Church
- The statue of Jesus Christ as a pharmacist in the Golden Eagle Pharmacy Museum
- The bombed-out Ministry of Defence, a casualty of WWII
- The restored altar of St John in the Hungarian National Gallery
- The Gothic statues at the Budapest History Museum

You can't avoid walking past the large Romantic-style **Matthias Fountain**, which portrays the young medieval King Matthias Corvinus in hunting garb and his admirer Szép Ilona (Beautiful Helen), a protagonist of a Romantic ballad by the poet Mihály Vörösmarty.

The most fun way to get to Castle Hill from Pest is to stroll across the Széchenyi Chain Bridge and board the **Sikló** (€ uphill/downhill 650/550Ft; ☉ 7.30am-10pm, closed 1st & 3rd Mon of each month), a funicular railway built in 1870 that ascends from Clark Ádám tér to Szent György tér near the Royal Palace.

The Fishermen's Bastion offers splendid views of the Danube and Pest

UNDERGROUND SECRETS

Sitting beneath Castle Hill is a 28km-long network of caves formed by thermal springs, which were supposedly used by the Turks for military purposes and served as air-raid shelters during WWII. They hid a secret military installation during the Cold War, and not without reason: the bombed-out Ministry of Defence, a casualty of WWII on the south side of Dísz tér, was apparently NATO's nuclear target for Budapest at the time.

THERMAL BATHS

Budapest is blessed with an abundance of hot springs – some 123 thermal and more than 400 mineral ones from 14 different sources. As a result, 'taking the waters' at one of the city's many thermal baths *(gyógyfürdő)* or combined spa-swimming pools is a unique Budapest experience, so try to go at least once. Some date from Turkish times, others are Art Nouveau wonders, while a few more are spick-and-span modern establishments.

All baths have cabins or lockers in which you store your belongings. Find a free one, get changed in (or at) it and call the attendant. They will lock the door with your clothes inside, write the time on a chalkboard on the door and hand you a numbered tag to tie on your costume. Note: in order to prevent theft lest you lose or misplace the tag, the number is not the same as the one on the locker, so commit the locker number to memory.

Though some of the local spas and baths look a little rough around the edges, they are clean and the water is changed regularly. You might consider taking along a pair of plastic sandals or flip-flops, however. Most bathhouses now require you to wear a bathing suit, and no longer distribute those strange drawstring loincloths. They usually hire out swimming costumes (for around 800Ft) if you don't have your own.

Generally, entry to those baths without a deposit or voucher system

Swimmers take the plunge in the grand Gellért Baths

(such as the Gellért, Rudas, Lukács and Széchenyi Baths), in which you get a refund if you leave two or three hours after you arrive, allows you to stay for two hours on weekdays and 1½ hours at weekends, though this rule is not always enforced. Most of the baths offer a full range of serious medical treatments, plus services such as massage (2000/3000Ft for 15/30 minutes) and pedicure (2500Ft). Specify what you want when buying your ticket.

Soaking in the resplendent Art Nouveau **Gellért Baths** has been likened to taking a bath in a cathedral. The pools maintain a constant temperature of 44°C, and the water, high in calcium, magnesium and hydrogen carbonate, is good for pains in the joints, arthritis and blood circulation. The entrance fee is actually a kind of deposit; you get back 600/300Ft if you leave within two/three hours of your arrival.

The **Király Baths** are genuine Turkish ones, erected in 1570. There's a wonderful skylit central dome over four pools, with water temperatures of between 26°C and 40°C.

Housed in a sprawling 19th-century complex, the **Lukács Baths** are popular with older, very keen spa aficionados, and include everything from thermal and mud baths (temperatures 22°C to 40°C) to a swimming pool. You get back 500/300Ft if you leave two/three hours after you enter.

The **Rudas Baths** are the most Turkish of all in Budapest, built in 1566, with an octagonal pool, domed skylit cupola and massive columns. On men's days only, you get back 700/400Ft if you leave two/three hours after you arrive.

The **Széchenyi Baths**, in the northern section of the City Park, are immense, with a dozen thermal baths and three swimming pools. Water temperatures are very hot (up to 38°C). You get back 600/300Ft if you leave within two/three hours of your arrival.

The **Thermal Baths**, in the Danubius Grand Hotel Margitsziget on leafy Margaret Island, are modern in style and offer lots of treatments. Come here if you favour cleanliness and modernity over atmosphere and history.

DON'T MISS

- The chess players at the Széchenyi
- The Art Nouveau pool at the Gellért
- The wonderful Turkish dome at the Rudas
- The famous mud baths at the Lukács
- A vigorous massage at any of the above

INFORMATION

An excellent overall source of information is the Budapest Spas and Hot Springs website: www.spasbudapest.com.

Gellért Baths (5, A6; ☎ 466 6166; XI Kelenhegyi út 4; 3000Ft; ☾ 6am-7pm Mon-Fri, 6am-5pm Sat & Sun May-Sep, 6am-7pm Mon-Fri, 6am-2pm Sat & Sun Oct-Apr; 🚊 18, 19, 47, 49)

Király Baths (4, C2; ☎ 202 3688, 201 4392; II Fő utca 84; 1100Ft; ☾ men 9am-8pm Tue, Thu & Sat, women 7am-6pm Mon, Wed & Fri; 🚌 60, 86)

Lukács Baths (4, C1; ☎ 326 1695; II Frankel Leó út 25-27; locker/cabin 1500/1700Ft; ☾ 6am-7pm daily May-Sep, 6am-7pm Mon-Fri, 6am-5pm Sat & Sun Oct-Apr; 🚊 17 or 🚌 60, 86)

Rudas Baths (5, A5; ☎ 356 1322, 356 1010; I Döbrentei tér 9; 2000Ft; ☾ men 6am-8pm Mon, Wed-Fri, women 6am-8pm Tues, mixed (bathing costume compulsory) 10pm-4am Fri, 8am-5pm & 10pm-4am Sat, 8am-5pm Sun; 🚊 18, 19 or 🚌 7, 86)

Széchenyi Baths (5, D1; ☎ 363 3210; XIV Állatkerti körút 11; locker/cabin 2000/2300Ft; ☾ 6am-7pm; Ⓜ M1 Széchenyi fürdő)

Thermal Baths (3, B3; ☎ 889 4737; ✉ XIII Margit-sziget; € weekday/weekend 5200/6300Ft; ☾ 6.30am-9.30pm; 🚌 26)

PARLIAMENT (5, A2)

The Eclectic-style Parliament, the symbol of Hungary's independence, was designed by Imre Steindl and completed in 1902. Visitors, who enter through Gate X (just one of 27 entrances), get to see three of the almost 700 sumptuously decorated rooms on a guided tour of the North Wing, notably the Domed Hall, where the **Crown of St Stephen**, the nation's most important national icon, is on display, along with the ceremonial sword, orb and the oldest object among the coronation regalia, the 10th-century sceptre with a crystal head depicting a lion made in what is now Iran. The two-part crown, with its characteristic cross set at a jaunty angle, pendants on either side hanging like earrings and enamelled plaques of the Apostles, dates from the 12th century. In addition, visitors pass through the Loge Hall and the Congress Hall, where the House of Lords of the one-time bicameral assembly sat until 1944.

The building is a blend of many architectural styles – neo-Gothic, neo-Romanesque, baroque – and, in sum, it works very well. Unfortunately, what was spent on the design was not matched by the building materials. The ornate structure was surfaced with a porous form of limestone that does not resist pollution very well at all. Renovations began almost immediately after it opened, and will continue until the day the building crumbles. Members of Parliament sit in the National Assembly Hall in the South Wing from February to June, and again from September to December.

INFORMATION

- ☎ 441 4904, 441 4415
- 🖵 www.mkogy.hu
- ✉ V Kossuth Lajos tér 1-3, Gate X
- € free for EU citizens, other nationalities 2300/1150Ft
- 🕑 8-11am Mon, 8am-6pm Tue-Sat, 8am-2pm Sun
- ⓘ English-language tours 10am, 12pm & 2pm daily; tours available in seven other languages
- Ⓜ M2 Kossuth Lajos tér
- ✗ Pozsonyi Kisvendéglő (p53)

The Parliament building, a national symbol of independence and statehood

A CROWN'S RANSOM

In 1945, Hungarian fascists fleeing the Soviet army took the Crown of St Stephen to Austria, where it eventually fell into the hands of the US Army and was sent to Fort Knox. In 1978, it was returned to Hungary with great ceremony. Because legal judgements had always been handed down 'in the name of St Stephen's Crown', it was considered a living symbol and had thus been 'kidnapped'.

BASILICA OF ST STEPHEN (5, B3)

Budapest's cathedral, the Basilica of St Stephen (Szent István Bazilika), was built over the course of half a century and not completed until 1905. Much of the interruption had to do with the fiasco in 1868 when the dome collapsed during a storm, and the structure had to be demolished and rebuilt from the ground up. The basilica is rather dark and soulless, but take a trip to the top of the **dome** (€ 500/400Ft; ☿ 10am-4.30pm Apr & May, 9.30am-6pm Jun-Aug, 10am-5.30pm Sep & Oct), reached by lift and 146 steps, for some of the best views in the city.

To the right as you enter the basilica is a small **treasury** (☿ 9am-5pm Apr-Sep, 10am-4pm Oct-Mar) of ecclesiastical objects and church plate. Behind the main altar and to the left is the basilica's major draw card: the **Holy Right Chapel** (☿ 9am-4.30pm Mon-Sat, 1-4.30pm Sun May-Sep, 10am-4pm Mon-Sat, 1-4.30pm Sun Oct-Apr). It contains the Holy Right (also known as the Holy Dexter), the mummified right hand of St Stephen and an object of great devotion. It was returned to Hungary by Habsburg Empress Maria Theresa in 1771 after it was discovered in a monastery in Bosnia. Like the Crown of St Stephen, it too was snatched by the bad guys after WWII, but was soon, er, handed over to the rightful owners.

INFORMATION

- ☎ 338 2151, 06 20 527 5329
- 🖥 www.basilica.hu
- ✉ V Szent István tér
- € free
- ☿ 9am-5pm & 7-8pm Mon-Fri, 9am-1pm & 7-8pm Sat, 1-5pm & 7-8pm Sun
- ⓘ English-language tours (2000/1500Ft with/without dome) 9.30am, 11am, 2pm & 3.30pm Mon-Fri, 9.30am & 11am Sat
- Ⓜ M2 Arany János utca
- ✂ Café Kör (p51)

SHAKE, RATTLE & ROLL

In 1996, in what must be one of the most bizarre 'reunions' of all times, the archbishop of Veszprém near Lake Balaton in central Hungary arranged for the hand and arm bone of King (St) Stephen's wife, Queen Gizella, to be sent to Hungary from Germany, so that it could lie in state with (and coyly touch) the Holy Right to mark the millennium of the royal couple's marriage.

Reliefs carved into the wall of the Basilica of St Stephen

MARGARET ISLAND (3, B4)

Neither Buda nor Pest, 2.5km-long Margaret Island (Margit-sziget) in the middle of the Danube was always the domain of one religious order or another until the Turks arrived and turned what was then called the Island of Rabbits into – appropriately enough – a harem, from which all infidels were banned. It's been a public park open to everyone since the mid-19th century.

Margaret Island is not overly endowed with important sights and landmarks, but with its large swimming complex, thermal spa, gardens and shaded walkways, the island is a lovely place to spend an afternoon away from the city. You can walk anywhere – on the paths, along the shoreline, on the grass.

INFORMATION
- ✉ XIII Margit-sziget
- € free
- ☽ 24hr
- 🚍 26 (between Nyugati train station & Árpád Bridge)
- ✂ Vogue (p54)

Close to the centre of the island are the ruins of a 13th-century **Franciscan church and monastery**, of which only the tower and a wall still stand. The **octagonal water tower** (1911), 600m to the northeast, rises above the **open-air theatre**, used for opera and plays in summer. Beyond the roundabout is the romantic **Japanese Garden**, with lily pads, carp and a small wooden bridge.

South of the **Danubius Grand Hotel Margitsziget** (p72), which has access to a thermal spa, is the reconstructed Romanesque **Premonstratensian Church** dedicated to St Michael. More ruins lie a few steps south. These are the remains of the former **Dominican convent** built by 13th-century King Béla IV, whose scribes played an important role in the continuation of medieval Hungarian scholarship.

GET THEE TO A NUNNERY
The Dominican convent's most famous resident was Béla's daughter, Margaret (1242–71). As the story goes, the king promised that his daughter would be committed to a life of devotion in a nunnery if the Mongols were driven from the land. They were and she was – at nine years of age. A red marble sepulchre cover marks her resting place.

MUSEUM OF FINE ARTS (5, D1)

The Museum of Fine Arts on the northern side of monumental Hősök tere contains Budapest's outstanding collection of foreign works in a renovated neoclassical building dating from 1906. The tympanum above the portico supports eight Corinthian columns. The relief shows centaurs doing battle with Lapiths, and is a copy of a similar scene at the Temple of Zeus in Olympia.

The **Old Masters Collection** is the most complete, with thousands of works from the Dutch and Flemish, Spanish, Italian, German and Austrian, French and British schools between the 13th and 18th centuries, including seven paintings by El Greco. In fact, the Spanish collection is the best and most complete outside Spain. Other sections include Egyptian and Graeco-Roman artefacts, and 19th- and 20th-century paintings, watercolours and graphics, and sculpture, including some notable impressionist works. Important temporary exhibits are staged in the Eclectic-style halls leading off from the entrance foyer.

The museum began life as a collection donated by Archbishop János Pyrker of Eger in northern Hungary, and was augmented by an extensive number of masterpieces purchased by the state at the end of the 19th century from the aristocratic Esterházy family. The museum underwent extensive renovations in the late 1990s and into the early part of the new millennium. Since then, the removal and rehanging of entire collections, beginning with the German and Austrian schools in 2003, has continued apace and should be complete by the time you read this.

INFORMATION

- ☎ 469 7100, 363 2675
- 🖳 www.szepmuveszeti.hu
- ✉ XIV Dózsa György út 41
- € Free temporary exhibitions 1200/600Ft
- ☽ 10am-5.30pm Tue-Sun
- ⓘ Free English-language tours 11am Tue-Sat
- Ⓜ M1 Hősök tere
- ✖ Bagolyvár (p56)

DON'T MISS

- *Portrait of a Man* (Albrecht Dürer)
- *The Eszterházy Madonna* (Raphael)
- *Peasants' Repast* (Diego Velázquez)
- *Lady with a Fan* (Édouard Manet)
- *Blue Village* (Marc Chagall)

HOUSE OF TERROR (5, C2)

Housed in the same building that served as headquarters of the pro-Nazi Arrow Cross Party from 1944 to 1945 (see p76) before being taken over by the dreaded ÁVH secret police during the communist regime, the House of Terror purports to focus on the crimes and atrocities committed by both Hungary's fascist and Stalinist regimes, but the latter, particularly in the years between WWII and the 1956 revolution, gets the lion's share of the exhibition space of almost three dozen rooms, halls and corridors over three floors.

INFORMATION

☎ 374 2600
🖥 www.terrorhaza.hu
✉ Andrássy út 60
€ 1500/750Ft
🕐 10am-6pm Tue-Fri, 10am-7.30pm Sat & Sun
Ⓜ M1 Vörösmarty utca
🍴 Menza (p53)

The museum was dismissed by many as a 'party-aligned piece of political propaganda' when it was opened by the centre-right Fidesz government in 2002, and it remains controversial, raising the question of which version of Hungarian history those in power would have you believe.

Highlights include the tank in the central courtyard, which provides a jarring introduction to the museum; the Changing Room, where a rotating dummy literally illustrates the ease with which some Hungarians were able to switch their allegiances to appease their new 'masters'; and taped testimony from one of the last resident executioners. The wall displaying many of the victims' photos speaks volumes, but even more harrowing are the reconstructed prison cells and the final Perpetrators' Gallery, featuring photographs of the turncoats, spies, torturers and 'cogs in the wheel', many of them still alive, who allowed or caused these atrocities to take place.

Delve into communist and fascist history at the House of Terror

LEST WE FORGET

Hungarian dissidents, of every size and hue, ended up at some stage at Andrássy út 60, where the walls were apparently of double thickness to mute the screams. A plaque on the outside of this house of shame reads in part: 'We cannot forget the horror of terror, and the victims will always be remembered.'

GREAT SYNAGOGUE (5, B4)

There are about half a dozen synagogues and prayer houses in the ghetto, the area of Pest once reserved for Jews, be they Conservative, Orthodox, Ashkenazic or Sephardic. But none compares with the Great Synagogue, the largest Jewish house of worship in the world outside New York. Built in 1859, it contains both Romantic and Moorish architectural elements. The copper-domed synagogue was renovated in the 1990s with funds raised by the Hungarian government and a New York-

INFORMATION
- ☎ 342 8949
- 🖳 www.bpjewmus.hu
- ✉ VII Dohány útca 2-8
- € synagogue 300Ft, synagogue & museum 1200/700Ft
- ☉ 10am-5pm Mon-Thu, 10am-2pm Fri & Sun mid-Apr–Oct, 10am-3pm Mon-Thu, 10am-3pm Fri, 10am-6pm Sun Nov–mid-Apr. English-language tours hourly 10.30am-1.30/3.30pm Mon-Thu, 10.30am-12.30pm Fri & Sun
- Ⓜ M2 Astoria
- ✗ Spinoza Café (p54)

DON'T MISS
- The 3rd-century gravestone with menorah from Roman Pannonia
- 18th-century hand-written and illuminated book of the Burial Society
- The Holocaust Memorial Room
- The renovated main organ, dating back to 1859
- The plaque for the birthplace of Theodor Herzl, the father of modern Zionism

based charity headed by the actor Tony Curtis, whose parents (family name: Kertész) emigrated from Hungary to the USA in the 1920s.

In an annexe of the synagogue, the **Jewish Museum** exhibits objects related to religious and everyday life, as well as 18th- and 19th-century art treasures in three main rooms. A fourth room is devoted to the Holocaust.

Imre Varga's 1989 **Holocaust Memorial**, on the Wesselényi utca side of the synagogue, stands over the mass graves of those murdered by Nazi and Arrow Cross supporters in 1944–45. On the leaves of the metal 'tree of life' are the family names of some of the 400,000 victims. In front of Dob utca 12, there's an unusual antifascist **monument to Carl Lutz**, a Swiss consul who, like Raoul Wallenberg (Budapest's Schindler; p21), provided Jews with false papers in 1944. It portrays an angel on high sending down a long bolt of cloth to a victim.

The Holocaust Memorial's metal 'tree of life' in front of the Great Synagogue

STATUE PARK (1, OFF A3)

Home to more than 40 busts, statues and plaques of Lenin, Marx, Engels and 'heroic' workers and communist martyrs that have ended up on trash heaps of history in most other former socialist countries, Statue Park is a truly mind-blowing place to visit. Ogle at the socialist realism, and try to imagine that at least four of these monstrous monuments were erected as recently as the late 1980s; a few of them, including the monument of socialist hero Béla Kun in a crowd by fence-sitting sculptor Imre Varga, were still in place when your humble author moved to Budapest in early 1992. The shop at the entrance sells a useful guidebook to the park and its sculptures, as well as fabulously kitsch communist memorabilia, statues, pins, CDs and 'the last breath of communism, sealed in a tin'.

INFORMATION

- ☎ 424 7500
- 🖥 www.szoborpark.hu
- ✉ cnr XXII Szabadkai út & Balatoni út
- € 600/400Ft
- ☉ 10am-dusk
- 🚌 Diósd-Érd bus from XI Etele tér terminus in south Buda

Communist sculptures in Statue Park

Socialist statues proliferated in Budapest as late as the early 1990s. The 14m-high **Independence Monument** (p27) on Gellért Hill was erected after the war in honour of the city's liberators, but the victims' names in Cyrillic letters on the plinth and the figures of the Soviet soldiers below were removed in 1992. And taking the place of the aforementioned Béla Kun monument in V Vértanúk tere is a striking **bronze of Imre Nagy**, the reformist communist prime minister executed for his role in the 1956 revolution (see p77).

A direct bus (2450/1950Ft) departs from V Deák Ferenc tér daily at 11am all year round, with an extra departure at 3pm in July and August.

BLOWING IN THE WIND

The Independence Monument was designed before WWII by the politically 'flexible' sculptor Zsigmond Kisfaludi Strobl for the ultra-right government of Admiral Miklós Horthy (see p76). After the war, when pro-communist monuments were in short supply, Kisfaludi Strobl passed it off as a memorial to the Soviets. It's now the much-loved 'Lady Liberty', proclaiming freedom throughout the land, and the city's unofficial symbol. And the beat goes on...

AQUINCUM (1, B1)

The most complete Roman civilian town in Hungary, and now an archaeological park and museum, Aquincum (see p75) had paved streets and fairly sumptuous single-storey houses with courtyards, fountains and mosaic floors, as well as sophisticated drainage and heating systems. The prosperous town's heyday was in the 2nd and 3rd centuries, lasting until the Huns and assorted other hordes came and ruined everything. The glory and grandeur are not all that apparent today as you walk among the ruins, but you can see the town's outlines as well as those of the big public baths, market, an early Christian church and a temple dedicated to the god Mithras,

DON'T MISS
- The replica of a 3rd-century portable water organ called a hydra
- The floor mosaics from the Roman governor's palace on Óbuda Island
- The mock-up of a Roman bath, with wall paintings and mosaics
- The stone effigy of Greek goddess Nemesis, symbol of divine retribution
- The remains of the *macellum*, the town's covered market

the chief deity of a religion that rivalled Christianity in its number of believers in the 2nd century AD. In the centre of what remains of the settlement, the five-room **Aquincum Museum**, with religious, decorative and everyday items on display in an attractive 19th-century neoclassical building, tries to put the ruins in perspective. Most of the big sculptures and stone sarcophagi are outside to the left of the museum or behind it in the lapidary.

Across Szentendrei út to the northwest is the **Roman Civilian Amphitheatre**. Much is left to the imagination, but you can still see the small cubicles where lions were kept and the 'Gate of Death' to the west through which slain gladiators were carried. An **aqueduct** dating from Roman times used to pass this way from a spring in a nearby park, and remains have been preserved in the central reservation (median strip) of Szentendrei út.

INFORMATION
- ☎ 250 1650, 430 1081
- 🖳 www.aquincum.hu
- ✉ III Szentendrei út 139
- € archaeological park 400/200Ft, park & museum 800/400Ft
- ⏱ park/museum 9/10am-6pm Tue-Sun May-Sep, 9/10am-5pm Tue-Sun 15-30 Apr & Oct
- 🚊 HÉV Aquincum

Sights & Activities

MUSEUMS

Applied Arts Museum (5, C5)

This stunning building, designed by Ödön Lechner, was completed for the Millenary Exhibition (1896). The galleries, which surround a central hall of white marble modelled on the Alhambra in southern Spain, usually contain a wonderful array of Hungarian furniture dating from the 18th and 19th centuries, Art Nouveau and Secessionist artefacts, and objects related to the history of arts and crafts. However, the last time I visited, there were only temporary exhibitions on display.
☎ 456 5100 🖳 www.imm.hu ✉ IX Üllői út 33-37 € free, temporary exhibitions 600/300Ft ☺ 10am-6pm Tue-Sun Ⓜ M3 Ferenc körút

Budapest History Museum (4, C5)

Also known as the Castle Museum, this place covers 2000 years of the city on three floors of rather jumbled exhibits. Restored palace rooms from the 15th century can be entered from the basement, which contains a display on the palace in medieval Buda. On the ground floor is an exhibition entitled 'Budapest in the Middle Ages', while the 1st floor traces the city's history from the expulsion of the Turks in 1686 to Hungary's entry into the EU.
☎ 225 7815, 375 7533 ✉ Royal Palace, Wing E € 900/450Ft, family 1500Ft, audioguide 800Ft ☺ 10am-6pm daily mid-May–mid-Sep, 10am-6pm Wed-Mon Mar–mid-May & mid-Sep–Oct, 10am-4pm Wed-Mon Nov-Feb 🚌 16 or Várbusz

Ethnography Museum (5, A2)

This museum offers an easy introduction to traditional Hungarian life, with thousands of displays in 13 rooms. The mock-ups of peasant houses from the Őrség and Sárköz regions of western and southern Transdanubia are well done, and there are some priceless objects collected from Transdanubia. The building was designed in 1893 to house the Supreme Court; note the ceiling fresco, *Justice*, by Károly Lotz.
☎ 473 2400 🖳 www.hem.hu ✉ V Kossuth Lajos tér 12 € free, temporary exhibitions 500/200Ft, family 1000Ft ☺ 10am-6pm Tue-Sun Ⓜ M2 Kossuth Lajos tér

Franz Liszt Memorial Museum (5, C2)

This is the building where the great composer lived in a 1st-floor apartment from 1881 until his death in 1886. The four rooms are filled with his pianos (including a tiny glass one), portraits and personal effects.
☎ 322 9804 ✉ VI Vörösmarty utca 35 € 400/250Ft ☺ 10am-6pm Mon-Fri, 9am-5pm Sat Ⓜ M1 Vörösmarty utca

Holocaust Memorial Center (5, D6)

This centre, opened in 2004 on the 60th anniversary of the start of the Holocaust in Hungary, displays pages from the harrowing 'Auschwitz Album', an unusual collection of photographs documenting the transport, internment and extermination of Hungarian Jews, found by a camp survivor after liberation. In the courtyard, a sublimely restored synagogue from 1924, designed by Leopold Baumhorn, hosts temporary exhibitions.
☎ 455 3348 🖳 www.hdke.hu ✉ IX Páva utca 39 € free ☺ 10am-6pm Tue-Sun Ⓜ M3 Ferenc körút

The white marble interior of the Applied Arts Museum

Hungarian National Museum (5, C5)

This large neoclassical structure purpose-built in 1847 contains Hungary's most important collection of historical relics. Look out for the enormous 3rd-century Roman mosaic from Balácapuszta, near Veszprém in central Transdanubia, at the foot of the central staircase; the crimson silk royal coronation robe; the reconstructed 3rd-century Roman villa from Pannonia; the treasury room with pre-conquest gold jewellery; a stunning baroque library; and Beethoven's Broadwood piano.

☎ 338 2122, 317 7806
🖳 www.mnm.hu
✉ VIII Múzeum körút 14-16 € free, temporary exhibitions 700/350Ft
🕑 10am-6pm Tue-Sun
🚊 47, 49

Hungarian Natural History Museum (5, E6)

This museum has lots of child-friendly hands-on interactive displays over three floors. The geological park in front of the museum is well designed, and there's an interesting exhibition focusing on both the natural resources of the Carpathian Basin and the flora and fauna of Hungarian legends and tales.

☎ 210 1085 🖳 www.nhmus.hu ✉ VIII Ludovika tér 2-6 € free, temporary exhibitions 1000/600Ft
🕑 10am-6pm Wed-Mon
Ⓜ M3 Klinikák

Kiscelli Museum & Municipal Gallery (4, off B1)

Housed in an 18th-century monastery, the exhibits at this museum tell the human side of the story of Budapest since liberation from the Turks. Among its best displays are a complete 19th-century apothecary moved here from Kálvin tér, ancient shop signs and rooms furnished with empire, Biedermeier and Art Nouveau furniture. The **Municipal Gallery** upstairs has an impressive art collection (József Rippl-Rónai, Lajos Tihanyi, István Csók, Béla Czóbel etc).

☎ 388 8560, 250 0304
✉ III Kiscelli utca 108
€ 600/300Ft, family 1000Ft 🕑 10am-6pm Tue-Sun Apr-Oct, 10am-4pm Nov-Mar 🚊 17

Military History Museum (4, A4)

Loaded with weaponry from before the Turkish conquest, the Military History Museum also has uniforms, medals, flags and battle-themed

BUDAPEST'S SCHINDLER

Of all the 'righteous gentiles' honoured by Jews around the world, the most respected is Raoul Wallenberg, the Swedish diplomat and businessman who rescued as many as 35,000 Hungarian Jews during WWII.

Sent to Budapest as an attaché to the Swedish embassy in 1944, Wallenberg immediately began issuing Swedish safe-conduct passes, and set up a series of 'safe houses' where Jews could find asylum. He even followed German 'death marches' and trains, distributing food and clothing, and actually pulling some 500 people out of the carriages.

When the Soviet army entered Budapest in January 1945, Wallenberg was arrested and sent to Moscow. In the early 1950s, the Soviet Union announced that he had died of a heart attack in 1947. Several reports over the next two decades suggested Wallenberg was still alive, but none was ever confirmed.

fine art. Exhibitions focus on the 1848–49 War of Independence and the Hungarian Royal Army under Admiral Miklós Horthy (1918–44).

☎ 356 9522 ✉ I Tóth Árpád sétány 40 € free ☑ 10am-6pm Tue-Sun Apr-Sep, 10am-4pm Tue-Sun Oct-Mar 🚌 16 or Várbusz

GALLERIES

House of Hungarian Photographers (5, B3)

The House of Hungarian Photographers is an interesting venue in the city's theatre district with top-class photography exhibitions. It is in delightful Mai Manó Ház, which was built in 1894 as a photography studio, and has the bizarre meaning 'Modern Devil House'.

☎ 473 2666 ✉ VI Nagymező utca 20 € 500/200Ft ☑ 2-7pm Mon-Fri, 11am-7pm Sat & Sun Ⓜ M1 Opera

Hungarian National Gallery (4, C5)

This massive collection of Hungarian art from the 10th century to the present day includes medieval and Renaissance stonework, Gothic wooden sculptures and winged altars, and late Renaissance and baroque art. The museum also has an important collection of Hungarian art from the 19th and 20th centuries; look out for the harrowing depictions of war by László Mednyánszky, the mammoth canvases by Tivadar Csontváry, the paintings of carnivals by Vilmos Aba-Novák and works by the

Miksa Róth's stunning stained glass; visit the museum of his life and work (opposite)

realist Mihály Munkácsy.

☎ 201 9082, 06 20 439 7325 ✉ Royal Palace, Wings B, C & D € free, special exhibitions 1500/800Ft, family 3000Ft ☑ 10am-6pm Tue-Sun 🚌 16 or Várbusz

Imre Varga Exhibition House (3, B1)

This space exhibits works by Imre Varga (1923–), one of Hungary's foremost sculptors, who seems for decades to have sat on both sides of the political fence – sculpting Béla Kun and Lenin as dexterously as he did St Stephen, Béla Bartók and even Imre Nagy. A short distance southwest of the museum is more of Varga's work: a group of metal sculptures of rather worried-looking women holding umbrellas.

☎ 250 0274 ✉ III Laktanya utca 7 € 500/250Ft ☑ 10am-6pm Tue-Sun 🚌 86

Kassák Museum (3, A1)

Sharing the same building as the Vasarely Museum (opposite) but facing the inner courtyard, the Kassák Museum contains some real gems of early-20th-century avant-garde art, as well as the complete works of the artist and writer Lajos Kassák (1887–1967). It is a three-hall art gallery on the 1st floor.

☎ 368 7021 ✉ III Fő tér 1 € free, temporary exhibitions 150/100Ft ☑ 10am-6pm Tue-Sun 🚌 86

Ludwig Museum of Contemporary Art (5, off C6)

Housed in the controversial Palace of Arts (Művészetek Palotája) opposite the National Theatre, this is Budapest's most important collection of contemporary art. It shows works by American, Russian, German and French artists from the past 50 years, and Hungarian, Czech, Slovakian, Romanian, Polish and Slovenian works from the 1990s onwards.

☎ 555 3444 🖳 www. ludwigmuseum.hu ✉ IX Komor Marcell utca 1 € free, temporary exhibitions 1000/500Ft ☑ 10am-6pm Tue, Fri & Sun, noon-6pm Wed,

noon-8pm Thu, 10am-8pm Sat ☎ 2

Miksa Róth Memorial House (5, D3)

This fabulous museum exhibits the work of the Art Nouveau stained-glass maker Miksa Róth (1865–1944) in the house and workshop where he lived and worked from 1911 until his death. Less well known are the master's stunning mosaics. Róth's dark brown, almost foreboding, living quarters stand in sharp contrast to the lively, technicolour creations that emerged from his workshop.

☎ 341 6789, 413 6147 ⊠ VII Nefelejcs utca 26 € 200/100Ft 🕒 2-6pm Tue-Sat Ⓜ M2 Keleti pályaudvar

Műcsarnok (5, D1)

Műcsarnok (Palace of Art) is among the city's largest exhibition spaces, and hosts temporary exhibitions of works by Hungarian and foreign artists in fine and applied art, photography and design. A 3-D film that whisks you around Hungary in 25 minutes (with commentary available in seven languages) is screened continuously from 10am to 5pm Tuesday to Sunday mid-March to September, and from 10am to 4.30pm Friday to Sunday from October to mid-March.

☎ 460 7014, 363 2671 💻 www.mucsar nok.hu ⊠ XIV Dózsa György út 37 € 3-D film 1000/500Ft, exhibitions & film 1500/500Ft 🕒 10am-6pm Tue-Sun Ⓜ M1 Hősök tere

Vasarely Museum (3, A1)

In the crumbling Zichy Mansion, this museum (part of the Museum of Fine Arts; (p15) contains the works of Viktor Vasarely (or Vásárhelyi Győző before he emigrated to Paris in 1930), the late 'father of op art'. The works, especially ones like *Dirac* and *Tlinko-F*, are excellent and fun to watch as they swell and move around the canvas. On the 1st floor are exhibitions of works by Hungarian artists based abroad.

☎ 388 7551 ⊠ III Szentlélek tér 6 € free, temporary exhibitions 400/200Ft 🕒 10am-5.30pm Tue-Sun 🚌 86

Zsigmond Kun Folk Art Collection (3, A1)

Most of the pottery and

BUDAPEST'S BRIDGES

The city's bridges, both landmarks and delightful vantage points over the Danube, have bound Buda and Pest together since well before the two were linked politically in 1873. The following stand head and shoulders above the rest.

Margaret Bridge (1876) Uniquely, it dog-legs in order to stand at right angles to the Danube at its confluence to the south of Margaret Island.

Széchenyi Chain Bridge (1849) When it opened, it was novel for two reasons: it was the first permanent dry link between Buda and Pest; and the aristocracy – previously exempt from all taxation – had to pay a toll like everybody else to use it.

Elizabeth Bridge (1964) It enjoys a special place in the hearts of many Budapesters, as the first newly designed bridge to reopen after WWII.

Liberty Bridge (1896) Opened for the 1896 millenary exhibition, it has a fin-de-siècle cantilevered span. Each post is topped by a mythical *turul* bird.

Quiet contemplation in the Cave Chapel

ceramics in this charming small museum are from Mezőtúr near the Tisza River, but there are some rare Moravian and Swabian pieces, as well as Transylvanian furniture and textiles. The attendants are very proud of the collection (housed in an 18th-century townhouse); be prepared for some lengthy explanations.
☎ 368 1138 ✉ III Fő tér 4 € 300/200Ft ☾ 10am-6pm Tue-Sun ☐ 86

PLACES OF WORSHIP

Cave Chapel (5, A5)
This chapel on a small hill north of the Gellért Hotel was built into a cave in 1926. It was the seat of the Pauline order until 1951, when the priests were arrested and imprisoned by the communists and the cave was sealed off. It was reopened and reconsecrated in 1992. Behind the chapel is the monastery, with its neo-Gothic turrets visible from Liberty Bridge.
☎ 385 1529 ☾ 9am-9pm ☐ 47, 49

Gül Baba's Tomb (4, B2)
This overly reconstructed tomb contains the remains of one Gül Baba, an Ottoman dervish who took part in the capture of Buda in 1541, and is known in Hungary as the 'Father of Roses'. The tomb is a pilgrimage place for Muslims, especially from Turkey, and you must remove your shoes before entering. There's a pleasant café here with fine views.
☎ 326 0062 ✉ II Türbe tér 1 € 500/250Ft ☾ 10am-6pm Mar-Oct,

10am-4pm Nov-Feb
☐ 17

Inner Town Parish Church (5, A4)
On the eastern side of Március 15 tér, sitting uncomfortably close to the Elizabeth Bridge flyover, is where a Romanesque church was first built in the 12th century within a Roman fortress. You can still see a few bits of the fort, Contra Aquincum, in the small park to the north. The present church was rebuilt in the 14th and 18th centuries, and you can spot Gothic, Renaissance, baroque and even Turkish elements both inside and out.
✉ V Március 15 tér 2 ☐ 2, 2A

Medieval Jewish Prayer House (4, B4)
With parts dating from the 14th century, this medieval Jewish house of worship contains documents and items linked to the Jewish community of Buda, as well as

A STREET BY ANY OTHER NAME
After WWII, most streets, squares and parks were renamed after people, dates and political groups that have since become anathema to an independent Hungary. For example, Ferenciek tere (Square of the Franciscans) was, until 1989, called Felszabadulás tér (Liberation Square), honouring the Soviet army's role in liberating Budapest at the end of the war. With the decline of the communist state, names were changed at a pace and with a determination that some people felt was almost obsessive; Cartographia's *Budapest Atlas* lists almost 400 street name changes in the capital alone. Sometimes, it was just a case of returning a street or square to its original (perhaps medieval) name – from Lenin útja, say, to Szent korona útja (Street of the Holy Crown). At other times, the name is completely new.

Detail of the Ferenc Liszt Academy of Music

Gothic stone carvings and tombstones from the Great Synagogue (p17) in Pest.
☎ 225 7815 ✉ I Táncsics Mihály utca 26 € 400/150Ft ☺ 10am-5pm Tue-Sun May-Oct 🚌 16 or Várbusz

NOTABLE BUILDINGS

Ferenc Liszt Academy of Music (5, C3)

The academy, designed by Kálmán Giergl and Flóris Korb in 1907, is interesting for its internal decorative elements – the dazzling Art Nouveau mosaic by Aladár Körösfői Kriesch, and some fine stained glass by master craftsman Miksa Róth (see p23). Also note the grid of laurel leaves below the ceiling, which mimics the ironwork dome of Vienna's Secession Building.
☎ 342 0179 🖳 www.zeneakademia.hu ✉ VI Liszt Ferenc tér 8 ☺ ticket office 10am-8pm Mon-Fri, 2-8pm Sat & Sun Ⓜ M1 Oktogon

Gresham Palace (5, A3)

This magnificent gold-tiled Art Nouveau building was built by an English insurance company in 1907. A major overhaul pieced back together the Zsolnay tiles, famous wrought-iron Peacock Gates and splendid mosaics, and it now houses the sumptuous Four Seasons Gresham Palace Hotel, arguably the city's finest (p71).
✉ V Roosevelt tér 5-6 Ⓜ M1 Vörösmarty tér 🚌 15 🚋 2, 2A

Hungarian State Opera House (5, B3)

The neo-Renaissance Hungarian State Opera House, among the city's most beautiful buildings, was designed by Miklós Ybl in 1884. If you cannot attend a concert or an opera, join one of the guided tours, which usually includes a brief musical performance. Tickets are available from the souvenir shop on the eastern side of the building facing Hajós utca.
☎ 332 8197 🖳 www.operavisit.hu ✉ VI Andrássy út 22 € 2400/1200Ft

☺ English-language tours 3pm & 4pm Ⓜ M1 Opera

National Theatre (1, B3)

The controversial design of this 2002 building, by Mária Siklós, is supposedly 'Eclectic' to mirror other great Budapest buildings of that style (Gellért Hotel, Gresham Palace, Parliament). But, in reality, it is a pick-and-mix jumble sale of classical and folk motifs, porticoes, balconies and columns. Particularly odd is the ziggurat-like structure outside whose ramps lead to nowhere.
☎ 476 6800 🖳 www.nemzeti szinhaz.hu ✉ IX Bajor Gizi park 1 🚋 2

Nyugati Train Station (5, B2)

The large iron and glass structure on Nyugati tér (known as Marx tér until the early 1990s) is Nyugati train station, built in 1877 by the Paris-based Eiffel Company. In the early 1970s, a train crashed through the enormous glass screen on the main façade when its brakes

FINDING BUDAPEST'S ART NOUVEAU TREASURES

One of the joys of exploring the 'Queen of the Danube' is that you'll find elements of Art Nouveau and Secessionism everywhere. Some people go out of their way for another glimpse of such 'hidden' favourites near the City Park as the **Geology Institute** (5, F2; XIV Stefánia út 14), designed by Ödön Lechner in 1899, or the **Philanthia** (5, A4; V Váci utca 9), a flower shop with an exquisite Art Nouveau interior (Kálmán Albert Körössy; 1906) in the Inner Town.

Other buildings worth a detour are the former **Török Bank House** (5, B4; V Szervita tér 3), designed by Henrik Böhm and Ármin Hegedűs in 1906, and sporting a wonderful Secessionist mosaic by Miksa Róth in the upper gable called *Patrona Hungariae*, depicting Hungary surrounded by great Hungarians of the past; Ármin Hegedűs' **primary school** (5, C3; VII Dob utca 85), built in the same year and with mosaics depicting contemporary children's games; and the delightful **City Park Calvinist Church** (5, D2; VII Városligeti fasor 7), a stunning example of late Art Nouveau architecture by Aladár Arkay (1913), with carved wooden gates, stained glass and ceramic tiles on the façade. **Bedő House** (5, A3; V Honvéd utca 3), an apartment block by Emil Vidor and completed in 1903, is one of the most intact Art Nouveau structures in the city. It contains some striking interior features, and the exterior (ironwork gate, majolica flowers, faces) has been renovated.

The style was hardly restricted to public buildings in Budapest, and the affluent districts to the west of the City Park are happy hunting grounds for some of the best examples of private residences built in the Art Nouveau/Secessionist style. The cream-coloured **Egger Villa** (5, D2; VII Városligeti fasor 24), designed by Emil Vidor in 1902, is among the purest – and most extravagant – examples of Art Nouveau in the city. On the other side of the road, the green **Vidor Villa** (5, D2; VII Városligeti fasor 33) with the curious turret was designed by Vidor for his father in 1905, and incorporates any number of European styles in vogue at the time, including French Art Nouveau and Japanese-style motifs. Other interesting buildings in this area are the **Lédere Mansion** (5, C2; VI Bajza utca 42), a block with mosaics built by Zoltán Bálint and Lajos Jámbor in 1902, and the **Sonnenberg Mansion** (5, C1; VI Munkácsy Mihály utca 23). Designed by Albert Körössy in 1903, it is now the headquarters of the Hungarian Democratic Forum (see p77).

TABÁN HISTORY

The leafy area between Gellért and Castle Hills known as the Tabán (4, C6) stretches northwest as far as Déli train station. It is associated with the Serbs, who settled here after fleeing from the Turks in the early 18th century. Plaques on I Döbrentei utca mark the water level of the Danube during two devastating floods in 1775 and 1838. The neighbourhood later became known for its restaurants and wine gardens – a kind of Montmartre for Budapest. Most of these burned to the ground at the turn of the 20th century. All that remains is a lovely little renovated building with a fountain, designed by Miklós Ybl in 1879, known as the **Castle Garden Kiosk** (Várkert Kioszk; I Ybl Miklós tér 2-6), which was once a pump house for Castle Hill and is now a casino.

failed, coming to rest at the 4 and 6 tram line.
☎ 349 0115 ✉ VI Teréz körút 55-57 Ⓜ M3 Nyugati pályaudvar

Royal Postal Savings Bank (5, B3)

The crowning glory of Secessionist master architect Ödön Lechner (1845–1914), and now part of the National Bank of Hungary, this is an extravaganza of floral mosaics, folk motifs and ceramic figures dating from 1901. The bull's head atop the central tower symbolises the nomadic past of the Magyars, while the ceramic bees scurrying up the pillars towards their hives represent organisation, industry and economy.
✉ V Hold utca 4 🚌 15

HISTORICAL SIGHTS & MONUMENTS

Citadella (5, A5)

Built by the Habsburgs after the 1848–49 War of Independence to 'defend' the city from further insurrection, by the time the Citadella was ready in 1851, the political climate had changed and it had become obsolete. It was given to the city in the 1890s, and parts of it were symbolically blown to pieces. Today the Citadella contains some big guns and dusty displays in the courtyard, a waxworks, a restaurant and a dance club.
☎ 365 6076 🖥 www.citadella.hu 🕙 24hr 🚌 27

Independence Monument (5, A5)

The charming lady with the palm frond proclaiming freedom throughout the city from atop Gellért Hill was erected in 1947 in tribute to the Soviet soldiers who died liberating Budapest in 1945. If you walk west for a few minutes along Citadella sétány north of the fortress, you'll come to what is arguably the best vantage point in Budapest.
Szabadság-szobor 🚌 27

Millenary Monument (5, D1)

Topping this 36m-high pillar is the Angel Gabriel, holding the Hungarian crown and a cross. At the base are Árpád and the six other Magyar chieftains who occupied the Carpathian Basin in the late 9th century. The 14 statues in the colonnades are of rulers and statesmen – starting with King Stephen on the left and ending with Lajos Kossuth on the right. The four allegorical figures atop are (from left to right): Work and Prosperity; War; Peace; Knowledge and Glory.
Ⓜ M1 Hősök tere

The Independence Monument on Gellért Hill

Shoes on the Danube (5, A3)

This new monument to Hungarian Jews shot and thrown into the Danube by members of the pro-Nazi Arrow Cross Party in 1944 is by Gyula Pauer. It's a simple affair – 60 pairs of old-style boots and shoes in cast iron, tossed higgledy-piggledy on to a bank of the river – but it is one of the most poignant monuments yet unveiled in this city of so many tears.

V Pesti alsó rakpart 🚋 2, 2A

PARKS & CEMETERIES

City Park (5, E1)

The Városliget (City Park) is Pest's green lung, an open space measuring almost a square kilometre that hosted most of the events during Hungary's 1000th anniversary celebrations in 1896. In general, museums lie to the south of XIV Kós Károly sétány, while venues of a less cerebral nature – including the Municipal Great Circus, Funfair Park and Széchenyi Baths – are to the north.

Ⓜ M1 Széchenyi fürdő

City Zoo & Botanical Garden (5, D1)

The zoo has a collection of some 3700 animals (big cats, rhinos, hippos), but some visitors come here just to look at the Secessionist animal houses built early in the 20th century, such as the **Elephant**

The domed Elephant House at the City Zoo is a big attraction

House (1912), with pachyderm heads in beetle-green Zsolnay ceramic, and the **Palm House** (admission 300Ft extra, including aquarium), erected by the Eiffel Company of Paris.

☎ 273 4900, 363 3701 🖳 www.zoobudapest. com ✉ XIV Állatkerti út 6-12 € 1300/900Ft, family 4100Ft ⏰ 9am-6.30pm Mon-Thu, 9am-7pm Fri-Sun May-Aug, shorter hours rest of year

Kerepes Cemetery (5, E4)

About 500m southeast of Keleti train station is the entrance to Budapest's equivalent of Père Lachaise cemetery in Paris, established in 1847. Some of the mausoleums are worthy of a pharaoh, especially those of statesmen and national heroes Lajos Kossuth, Ferenc Deák and Lajos Batthyány. Other tombs are quite moving, like those of actress Lujza Blaha and poet Endre Ady. Plot 21 contains the graves of many who died in the 1956 revolution.

☎ 333 9125, 314 1269 ✉ VIII Fiumei út 16 ⏰ 7am-8pm May-Jul, 7am-7pm Apr & Aug, 7am-6pm Sep, 7am-5pm Oct-Mar 🚋 24

CITY PARK STATUES & MONUMENTS

City Park boasts a number of notable statues and monuments. Americans will be amused to see a familiar face in the park south of the lake. The **George Washington Statue** (5, E1) was erected by Hungarian Americans in 1906. The little church opposite Vajdahunyad Castle (housing the Agricultural Museum) is called **Ják Chapel** because its intricate portal was copied from the 13th-century Abbey Church in Ják in western Transdanubia. The statue of the hooded figure south of the chapel is that of **Anonymous**, the unknown chronicler at the court of King Béla III who wrote a history of the early Magyars. Note the pen with the shiny tip in his hand; writers (both real and aspirant) touch it for inspiration.

QUIRKY BUDAPEST

Agricultural Museum (5, E1)

This rather esoteric museum is housed in the stunning baroque wing of Vajdahunyad Castle, built for the 1896 millenary celebrations on the little island in the lake of the City Park, and modelled after a fortress in Transylvania. Here you'll find Europe's largest collection of things agricultural.

☎ 422 0765, 363 1117
▣ www.mmgm.hu
✉ XIV Vajdahunyad sétány € free, temporary exhibitions 550/300Ft
☼ 10am-5pm Tue-Sun mid-Feb–mid-Nov, 10am-4pm Tue-Fri, 10am-5pm Sat & Sun mid-Nov–mid-Feb Ⓜ M1 Hősök tere

Electrotechnology Museum (5, C4)

This museum has a collection of 19th-century generators, condensers and motors, and the world's largest supply of electricity-consumption meters. The enthusiastic staff will show you how the alarm system of the barbed-wire fence between Hungary and Austria once worked. There's also a display on the nesting platforms that the electric company kindly builds for storks, so they won't try to nest on the wires and electrocute themselves.

☎ 322 0472 ✉ VII Kazinczy utca 21 € free
☼ 11am-5pm Tue-Sat Ⓜ M2 Astoria

Golden Eagle Pharmacy Museum (4, B4)

Just north of Dísz tér on the site of Budapest's first pharmacy (1681), this branch of the Semmelweis Museum of Medical History contains an unusual mixture of displays, including a mock-up of an alchemist's laboratory and a small 'spice rack' used by 17th-century travellers for their daily fixes of herbs.

☎ 375 9772 ✉ I Tárnok utca 18 € free
☼ 10.30am-5.30pm Tue-Sun mid-Mar–Oct, 10.30am-3.30pm Tue-Sun Nov–mid-Mar 🚌 16 or Várbusz

LIFT US THIS DAY

One of the strangest public conveyances you'll ever encounter can still be found in a few office buildings in Budapest. They're the *körforgó* (rotator) lifts or elevators, nicknamed 'Pater Nosters' for their supposed resemblance to a large rosary. A Pater Noster is essentially a rotating series of individual cubicles that runs continuously. You don't push a button and wait for a door to open; you hop on just as a cubicle reaches floor level and you jump out – quickly – when you reach your desired floor. When it reaches the top, the lift simply descends to the ground floor in darkness to begin its next revolution. The most central Pater Noster – that you may or may not be able to ride – is in the government building at V Vigadó utca 6 (5, A4).

Vajdahunyad Castle, home to the Agricultural Museum

Museum of Commerce & Catering (4, B4)

The catering section of this museum, to the left as you enter the archway, contains an entire 19th-century cake shop in one of its three rooms, complete with a pastry kitchen. There are moulds for every occasion, a marble-lined icebox and an antique ice-cream maker. The commerce collection traces retail trade in the capital. Along with advertisements and electric toys that still work, there's an exhibition on the hyperinflation that Hungary suffered after WWII when a basket of money would buy no more than four eggs.
☎ 375 6249 ⊠ I Fortuna utca 4 € 400/200Ft, family 1000Ft ⊗ 10am-5pm Wed-Fri, 10am-6pm Sat & Sun 🚌 16 or Várbusz

BUDAPEST FOR CHILDREN

Budapest Eye (5, B2)

This attraction exaggerates just a titch when it claims, 'The Budapest Eye is to Budapest what the Eiffel Tower is to Paris and the London Eye is to London.' In reality, it's a hot-air balloon tethered to ropes, on a site between Nyugati train station and the West End City Center mall, which ascends to 150m for some hair-raising views over Budapest. But the kids will love it.
☎ 238 7623 ⊠ VI Váci út 1-3 € 3000/1000Ft, family 6000Ft ⊗ 10am-10pm Sun-Thu, 10am-midnight Sat Ⓜ M3 Nyugati pályaudvar

Budapest Puppet Theatre (5, C2)

The puppet theatre, which usually doesn't require fluency in Hungarian, presents shows designed for children on weekdays (usually at 10am or 10.30am and 4pm) and folk programmes for adults occasionally in the evening.
☎ 342 2702, 321 5200 🖳 www.budapest-babszinhaz.hu ⊠ VI Andrássy út 69 € 500-1100Ft Ⓜ M1 Vörösmarty utca

Funfair Park (5, E1)

This 150-year-old amusement park has two dozen thrilling rides, including the heart-stopping Ikarus Space Needle, the looping Star roller coaster and the Hip-Hop freefall tower, as well as go-karts, dodgem cars and a merry-go-round built in 1906.
☎ 363 8310, 363 2660 🖳 www.vidampark.hu ⊠ XIV Állatkerti körút 14-16 € admission 300Ft, rides 300-600Ft ⊗ 10am-8pm daily Jul & Aug, 11am-7pm Mon-Fri, 10am-8pm Sat & Sun May & Jun, shorter hours rest of year Ⓜ M1 Széchenyi fürdő

Municipal Great Circus (5, D1)

Performances at Budapest's circus, Europe's only permanent big top, are at 3pm from Wednesday to Sunday, with additional shows at 10.30am on Saturday and Sunday, and at 7pm on Saturday.
☎ 344 6008, 343 8300 🖳 www.maciva.hu in Hungarian ⊠ XIV Állatkerti körút 7 € 1200-1900Ft/900-1500Ft Ⓜ M1 Széchenyi fürdő

Palace of Miracles (5, off C1)

This is a wonderfully thought-out interactive playhouse for children of all ages with 'smart' toys and puzzles, most of which have a scientific bent.
☎ 350 6131 🖳 www.csodapalota.hu ⊠ XIII Váci út 19 € 800/700Ft, family 2300Ft ⊗ 10am-6pm Jul & Aug, 9am-5pm Mon-Fri, 10am-6pm Sat & Sun Sep-Jun Ⓜ M3 Lehel tér

A mural at the Municipal Great Circus

Trips & Tours

WALKING TOURS
Castle Hill Stroll

Start by walking up Várfok utca from Moszkva tér to the **Vienna Gate** (**1**), the medieval entrance to the Old Town. The large building with the superb majolica-tiled roof contains the **National Archives** (**2**), built in 1920. On the west side of the square (a weekend market in the Middle Ages) is a group of **burgher houses** (**3**).

Architecture along Fortuna utca

Walk down Táncsics Mihály utca. In the entrances to many of the courtyards are *sedilia* – stone niches dating as far back as the 13th century. The **Medieval Jewish Prayer House** (**4**; p24) contains a small museum. The controversial **Hilton Budapest** (**5**), which incorporates parts of a medieval Dominican church and a baroque Jesuit college, is further south.

Distance 2km Duration 1.5hr
▶ Start II Moszkva tér
● End Hungarian National Gallery

Back up Fortuna utca is Kapisztrán tér; the steeple to the south is **Mary Magdalene Tower** (**6**), the reconstructed spire of an 18th-century church. Now walk southeast along Úri utca, which has some interesting courtyards, especially at No 19; there are more Gothic *sedilia* at Nos 32 and 40. Stop at **Ruszwurm** (**7**; p61) for a coffee. Szentháromság tér is dominated by **Matthias Church** (**8**; p8) and the **Fishermen's Bastion** (**9**; p9). Continue to Dísz tér, then south to Szent György tér. You'll pass the **former Ministry of Defence** (**10**) on the right, and on the left the restored **Sándor Palace** (**11**), which now houses the offices of the president.

The **Habsburg Steps** (**12**) are flanked by the **statue of the turul** (**13**), a totemic bird of the ancient Magyars, from 1905. Enter the Royal Palace via **Corvinus Gate** (**14**), where you'll find the **Hungarian National Gallery** (**15**; p22).

Explore the Inner Town

Start at **Egyetem tér** (**1**), a five-minute walk south along Károlyi Mihály utca from Ferenciek tere. North is the neoclassical **Károly Palace** (**2**) of 1840, housing a museum, library and terrace restaurant (see p49). To the west is the **University Church** (**3**), a baroque structure from 1748. North off Cukor utca is **Szivárvány köz** (**4**), the narrowest and shortest street in Budapest. The building with the multicoloured tiled dome north of the alley is the **Loránd Eötvös University Library** (**5**).

Don't miss the fabulous mosaic on the façade of the Török Bank House

To get to Váci utca from Ferenciek tere, walk through **Párisi Udvar** (**6**), a Parisian-style arcade built in 1909. Make a detour off Váci utca on to Haris köz, once a privately owned street, and continue across Petőfi Sándor utca to **Kamermayer Károly tér** (**7**), a lovely square. On the southeastern corner is the **Pest county hall** (**8**), a large neoclassical building with three courtyards. North of the square is the 18th-century **municipal council office** (**9**), or city hall, the largest baroque building in the city.

Opposite **Szervita tér** (**10**), at the northwestern end of Városház utca, is the 1912 apartment block **Rózsavölgyi House** (**11**), an example of early Modernism; and the former **Török Bank House** (**12**; p26) – look up for the marvellous mosaic. Back on Váci utca, many buildings are worth a closer look, including **Thonet House** (**13**), a masterpiece by Ödön Lechner (1890).

Váci utca leads into **Vörösmarty tér** (**14**), in the centre of which is a statue of the eponymous 19th-century poet, and at the northern end is **Gerbeaud** (**15**; p61), Budapest's most famous café and cake shop.

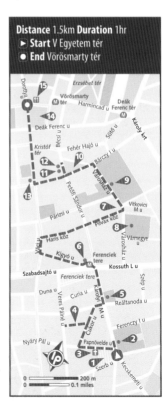

Distance 1.5km **Duration** 1hr
▶ **Start** V Egyetem tér
● **End** Vörösmarty tér

Up Andrássy út

The first major point is the **Hungarian State Opera House** (**1**; p25), the interior of which sparkles following its 1980s overhaul. Opposite, **Drechsler House** (**2**) was designed by Art Nouveau master builder Ödön Lechner in 1882. Down Dalszínház utca is the magical **New Theatre** (**3**), a Secessionist gem embellished with monkey faces and geometric designs that opened as a music hall in 1909.

Nagymező utca, 'the Broadway of Budapest', counts a number of theatres, including the **Budapest Operetta** (**4**; p67) and the **Thália** (**5**), lovingly restored in 1997. On the next block, the **Fashion House** (**6**) was the fanciest emporium in town when it opened as the Grande Parisienne in 1912. The Ceremonial Hall on the mezzanine floor is dripping with gilt and frescoes by Károly Lotz.

Just beyond Oktogon is the former secret police building now housing the **House of Terror** (**7**; p16). Along the next two blocks you'll pass some very grand buildings housing such institutions as the **Budapest Puppet Theatre** (**8**; p30) at No 69, the **Academy of Fine Arts** (**9**) next door and the headquarters of **MÁV** (**10**), the national railway, after that. The next square is **Kodály körönd** (**11**), one of the most beautiful in the city.

Andrássy út ends at **Hősök tere** (Heroes' Square; **12**), with the flamboyant **Millenary Monument** (**13**; p27).

Distance 2km **Duration** 1.5hr
- ▶ **Start** Opera metro station
- ● **End** VI Hősök tere

The spectacular State Opera House

Walk the Jewish Quarter

At the southeastern end of Liszt Ferenc tér, you'll find the magnificent **Ferenc Liszt Academy of Music** (**1**; p25). Southwest along Király utca is the **Church of St Teresa** (**2**) from 1811 and, diagonally opposite, a lovely **neo-Gothic house** (**3**) at No 47, built in 1847.

A couple of streets southeast over Dob utca is **Klauzál tér** (**4**), the heart of the old Jewish Quarter. The surrounding streets retain a feeling of prewar Budapest; look for the kosher bakery at Kazinczy utca 28, the Kővári butcher's at Dob utca 35, the Fröhlich cake shop and café at Dob utca 22and the wigmaker's at Kazinczy utca 32.

There are about half a dozen synagogues and prayer houses in the Erzsébetváros district. The **Orthodox Synagogue** (**5**) was built in 1913, and the Moorish **Rumbach Sebestyén utca Synagogue** (**6**) in 1872 by Austrian Secessionist architect Otto Wagner. But none compares with the **Great Synagogue** (**7**), which also contains the **Jewish Museum** (**8**; p17). Outside, a plaque notes that Theodor Herzl, the father of

Patterns on the Great Synagogue's façade

modern Zionism, was born at this site in 1860. The **Holocaust Memorial Center** (**9**; p20) is on the northern side of the synagogue.

Walk south to **Rákóczi út** (**10**), a busy shopping street, which leads to **Blaha Lujza tér** (**11**). The subway (underpass) below is one of the liveliest in the city, with hustlers, beggars, musicians and pickpockets. North is the Art Nouveau **New York Palace** (**12**), former home of the celebrated New York Café, and now the most gilt-edged coffee stop in town.

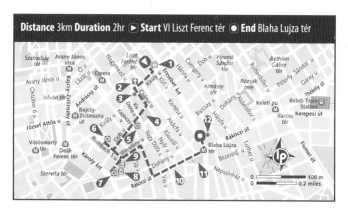

Distance 3km **Duration** 2hr ▶ **Start** VI Liszt Ferenc tér ● **End** Blaha Lujza tér

DAY TRIPS
Szentendre

Szentendre, an art colony turned tourist centre, has changed little in appearance since the 18th century. Its cobblestone-paved alleyways and skyline of church spires, as well as its many art museums and galleries, make the trip well worthwhile – but try to avoid it on summer weekends.

In the centre of **Fő tér**, the colourful heart of Szentendre surrounded by 18th- and 19th-century burghers' houses, stands the **Plague Cross** (1763), an iron cross decorated with icons. Across the square is the Serbian Orthodox **Blagoveštenska Church** (1754). With fine baroque and rococo elements, it hardly looks 'eastern' from the outside, but the ornate iconostasis and elaborate 18th-century furnishings inside give it away.

The **Margit Kovács Ceramic Collection** contains works by Kovács (1902–77), a ceramicist who combined Hungarian folk, religious and modern themes to create elongated, Gothic-like figures.

Castle Hill was the site of a fortress in the Middle Ages, but all that's left of it is the **Parish Church of St John**, with great views of the town. The red spire of **Belgrade Cathedral** (1764), seat of the Serbian Orthodox bishop in Hungary, rises from within a walled courtyard. One of the church outbuildings contains the **Serbian Ecclesiastical Art Collection**, a treasure-trove of icons, vestments and other sacred objects in precious metals.

INFORMATION
19km north of Budapest

🚢 From May to Sep, daily Mahart ferries to/from Vigadó tér (5, A4) in Pest and Batthyány tér (4, C3) in Buda (2hr; single/return 990/1485Ft); weekends only in Apr, late Sep & Oct

🚃 HÉV trains depart from Batthyány tér (4, C3) in Buda (40min; 160Ft) every 10-20 min daily

☎ 26 317 965

🖳 szentendre@tourinform.hu

€ Belgrade Cathedral 300/150Ft; Blagoveštenska Church 200Ft; Margit Kovács Ceramic Collection 600/300Ft; Serbian Ecclesiastical Art Collection 400/200Ft

🕓 Belgrade Cathedral 10am-6pm Tue-Sun Mar-Oct, shorter hours Jan & Feb; Blagoveštenska Church 10am-5pm Tue-Sun; Margit Kovács Ceramic Collection 9am-5pm Mar, 10am-6pm Apr-Oct; Parish Church of St John 10am-4pm Tue-Sun Apr-Oct; Serbian Ecclesiastical Art Collection 10am-6pm Tue-Sun Mar-Oct, 10am-4pm Fri-Sun Jan & Feb

ℹ Tourinform (Dumtsa Jenő utca 22); open 9.30am-4.30pm Mon-Fri all year round, 10am-2pm Sat & Sun mid-Mar–Oct

Gödöllő

The main attraction of Gödöllő ('gird-duh-ler') is the **Royal Mansion**, Hungary's largest baroque manor house, completed in the 1760s. But the town of Gödöllő itself, full of lovely baroque buildings and monuments, and home to the seminal Gödöllő artists' colony of 1901–20, is worth the trip.

The Royal Mansion was designed by András Mayerhoffer in 1741. After the formation of the Dual Monarchy in 1867, it was enlarged as a summer retreat for Emperor Franz Josef and soon became the favoured residence of his consort, the beloved Habsburg empress Elizabeth, or Sissi (1837–98). Between the two world wars, the regent, Admiral Miklós Horthy, used it as a summer residence, but after the communists came to power, part of the mansion was used as a Soviet barracks, then subsequently as an old people's home. The rest was left to decay.

Partial renovation of the mansion began in 1994, and today there are 26 rooms open for public inspection on the ground and 1st floors. They have been restored to the period when the imperial couple were in residence, and Franz Josef's suites and Sissi's lavender-coloured private apartments are impressive. Check out the **Decorative Hall**, all gold tracery and chandeliers, where chamber-music concerts are held all year round (especially in June and July during the Palace Concerts Chamber Music Festival); the **Queen's Salon**, with a Romantic-style oil painting of Sissi repairing the coronation robe of King Stephen; and the **Study Annexe**, with an 18th-century tapestry of the huntress Diana.

INFORMATION
27km northeast of Budapest

- 🚆 HÉV trains depart from Örs vezér tere at the terminus of the M2 metro (40 min; 326Ft) every half hour daily; get off at Szabadság tér
- ☎ 28 415 402
- 🖥 www.godollotourinform. hu; www.kiralyikastely.hu
- € Royal Mansion 1400/700Ft
- 🕙 Royal Mansion 10am-6pm Tue-Sun Apr-Oct, 10am-5pm Tue-Sun Nov-Mar
- ℹ Tourinform (just inside the entrance to the Royal Mansion); open 10am-6pm Tue-Sun Apr-Oct, 10am-5pm Tue-Sun Nov-Mar

ORGANISED TOURS

Absolute Walking Tours (5, B4)
This very reliable outfit has a 3½-hour guided promenade through the City Park, central Pest and Castle Hill. Tours depart from the steps of the yellow church on V Deák Ferenc tér (5, B4). Cracking specialist tours include the Hammer & Sickle Tour and the Hungaro Gastro Food & Wine Tour.
☎ 266 8777, 06 30 211 8861 ⌨ www.absolutetours.com
✉ V Sütő utca 2 € 4000/3500Ft ⏱ 9.30am & 1.30pm daily mid-May–Sep; 10.30am daily rest of year

Budatours (5, B3)
Budatours runs nine city bus tours daily in both open and covered coaches in July and August (between three and eight the rest of the year). It's a two-hour tour with one stop (Gellért Hill) and with taped commentary in 16 languages.
☎ 353 0558, 374 7070 ⌨ www.budatours.hu
✉ VI Andrássy út 2 € 4300/3000Ft per adult/student

Hungária Koncert
Focusing on Budapest's Jewish heritage, this operator has a 2½-hour tour including the Great and Orthodox Synagogues, the Jewish Museum and a walking tour of the ghetto. Tickets are available from locations throughout the city, including at the entrance to the Great Synagogue (5, B4; VII Dohány utca 2-8).

☎ 317 2754, 201 5928 ⌨ www.ticket.info.hu
€ 5600Ft includes nonkosher snack
⏱ 10.30am & 1.30pm most weekdays, 11.30am Sun

Legenda (5, A4)
A long-established operator offering boat cruises on the Danube, with taped commentary in up to 30 languages. The night lights of the city rising to Buda Castle, Parliament, Gellért Hill and the Citadella make the evening trip far more attractive than the afternoon one.
☎ 317 2203, 06 30 944 5216 ⌨ www.legenda.hu
✉ V Vigadó tér, pier 7
€ day/night tour 3600/4200Ft

Paul Street Tours
These very personal walking tours cover Castle Hill, less-explored areas of Pest, such as the Jewish Quarter and Andrássy út, Budapest's

parks and gardens, and shopping, with lots of information on architecture and social history, especially life in fin-de-siècle Pest. Tours are available in English or Hungarian.
☎ 06 20 933 5240 ⌨ taylorj@mail.datanet.hu
€ €25 per hour regardless of size ⏱ by appointment

Yellow Zebra Bikes (5, B3)
Run by the same people behind Absolute Walking Tours, Yellow Zebra has cycling tours taking in Heroes' Square, the City Park, inner Pest and Castle Hill. They depart from in front of the yellow Calvinist church in V Deák Ferenc tér, and last 3½ to four hours.
☎ 266 8777, 06 30 211 8861 ⌨ www.yellowzebrabikes.com
✉ V Sütő utca 2
€ 5500Ft includes bike & drink ⏱ 11am May-Oct, plus 4pm Jul & Aug

Tired feet can jump on a tram from Blaja Lujza tér

Shopping

Head to the Great Market, Nagycsarnok (opposite), for fabulous food

Traditional markets in Budapest stand side by side with mammoth shopping malls, and old-style umbrella or button makers can be found next to cutting-edge fashion boutiques. Traditional items include folk embroidery and ceramics, pottery, wall hangings, painted wooden toys and boxes, dolls, all types of basketry, and porcelain (especially from Herend and Zsolnay). Feather or goose-down pillows and duvets (comforters) are of exceptionally high quality.

Foodstuffs that are expensive or difficult to buy elsewhere – goose liver (both fresh and potted), saffron, dried forest mushrooms, jam (especially the apricot variety), prepared meats like Pick salami, the many types of paprika – make nice gifts (as long as you're allowed to take them home). Some of Hungary's 'boutique' wines (see p41) can be good and relatively inexpensive presents; a bottle of six-*puttonyos* Tokaji Aszú dessert wine always goes down a treat. Fruit-flavoured *pálinka* (brandy) is a stronger option.

Very generally speaking, retail shops and department stores are open from 10am to 6pm on Monday to Friday, and from 10am to 1pm on Saturday. In summer, some private retail shops close early on Friday and during at least part of August.

If you're not a resident of the EU, you can get an ÁFA (VAT or sales tax) refund, provided you have spent more than 50,000Ft in any one shop and take the goods out of the country (and the EU) within 90 days. The ÁFA receipts (available from the shops where you make the purchases) should be stamped by customs at the border, and the claim has to be made within 183 days of exporting the goods. You can collect your refund from **Global Refund** (www.global refund.com).

SHOPPING STREETS & AREAS
V Falk Miksa utca (Pest, 5, A2) Antiques
II Frankel Leó út (Buda, 4, B2) Antiques
V Múzeum körút (Pest, 5, B4) Antiquarian and secondhand bookshops
V Váci utca (Pest, 5, B5) Top-end boutiques and tourist schlock

MARKETS

If you don't have time to get to one of Budapest's excellent flea markets, check out one of the **BÁV** stores (p42).

City Park Flea Market
(5, E1)
This is a huge outdoor flea market – a kind of Hungarian boot or garage sale – where you'll find diamonds-to-rust stuff, from old records and draperies to candles, honey and herbs. Sunday is the better day.
☎ 363 3730, 251 7266
🖳 www.bolhapiac.com
✉ XIV Zichy Mihály út
🕑 7am-2pm Sat & Sun
🚃 1, 1A

Ecseri Piac (5, off E6)
Often just called the *piac* (market), this is one of the biggest and best flea markets in Central Europe, selling everything from antique jewellery and Soviet army watches to old musical instruments and Fred Astaire-style top hats. Saturday is the best day to go. To get there, take bus 54 from Boráros tér in Pest near Petőfi Bridge or, better yet, the red express bus 54 from the Határ utca stop on the M3 metro line and get off at the Fiume utca stop. Then follow the crowds over the pedestrian bridge.
☎ 282 9563 ✉ XIX Nagykőrösi út 🕑 8am-4pm Mon-Fri, 6am-3pm Sat, 8am-1pm Sun 🚌 54

Nagycsarnok (5, B5)
The 'Great Market' is Budapest's biggest food market; since being renovated in 1996, it also has dozens of stalls on the 1st floor's south side selling Hungarian folk costumes and handicrafts. Gourmets will appreciate the shrink-wrapped and potted foie gras, a good selection of dried mushrooms, garlands of dried paprika, sacks and tins of paprika powder, and as many types of honey and wine as you'd care to name – available on the ground floor at a fraction of what they would cost in the shops on Váci utca.
✉ IX Vámház körút 1-3
🕑 6am-5pm Mon, 6am-6pm Tue-Fri, 6am-2pm Sat
🚃 47, 49

MALL MADNESS

Hungarians call them *bevásárló és szórakoztató központ* (shopping and amusement centres); perhaps a more accurate description of places where you'll find everything from designer salons and traditional shops to food courts, casinos and multiplex cinemas. Central malls are **Mammut** (4, A3; ☎ 345 8020; II Lövőház utca; 🕑 8am-11pm) in Buda – actually two 'Mammoths' side by side – with almost as many fitness centres, billiard parlours, dance clubs and cafés as shops; and in central Pest **West End City Centre** (5, B2; ☎ 238 7777; VI Váci út 1; 🕑 8am-11pm), with 400 shops, indoor fountains and the hair-raising Budapest Eye (p30).

PORCELAIN & GLASSWARE

Ajka Kristály (5, B2)
Established in 1878, Ajka has Hungarian-made lead-crystal pieces and stemware. Most of it is very old-fashioned, but there are some more contemporary pieces.
☎ 332 4541 ✉ VI Teréz körút 50 Ⓜ M3 Nyugati pályaudvar

Haas & Czjzek (5, B3)
In the vicinity of the Basilica of St Stephen, this chinaware and crystal shop sells Zsolnay as well as more affordable Hungarian-made Hollóháza and Alföldi porcelain.
☎ 311 4094 🖳 www.porcelan.hu ✉ VI Bajcsy-Zsilinszky út 23 🕑 10am-7pm Mon-Fri, 10am-3pm Sat Ⓜ M3 Arany János utca

Herend (4, B4)
For fine porcelain, Herend is Hungary's answer to Wedgwood. Among the most popular motifs is

Hungarian porcelain and giftware at Zsolnay

the Victorian pattern of butterflies and wildflowers designed for the eponymous British queen in the mid-19th century. There's also a more central Belváros branch (5, A4; ☎ 317 2622; V József nádor tér 11).
☎ 225 1050 🖳 www.herend.com ✉ I Szentháromság utca 5 🕑 10am-6pm Mon-Fri, 9am-1pm Sat & Sun 🚌 16 or Várbusz

HEREND PORCELAIN

Herend porcelain is among the finest of goods produced in Hungary. A terracotta factory was set up in Herend (near Veszprém) in 1826, and began producing porcelain 13 years later. Initially it specialised in copying and replacing the nobles' broken chinaware settings imported from Asia, but soon began producing its own patterns; many, like the Rothschild bird and petites roses, were inspired by Meissen and Sèvres designs from Germany and France.

To avoid bankruptcy in the 1870s, the factory began mass production; tastes ran from kitschy pastoral scenes to the animal figurines with distinctive scale-like triangle patterns still popular today. In 1993, 75% of the factory was purchased by its 1500 workers, and became one of the first companies in Hungary privatised through an employee share-ownership plan.

Herend Village Pottery (4, C3)
An alternative to what some might call the overwrought Herend porcelain is the hard-wearing Herend pottery and dishes decorated with bold fruit patterns sold here. You can also enter from II Fő utca 61.
☎ 356 7899 ✉ II Bem rakpart 37 🕑 9am-5pm Mon-Fri, 9am-noon Sat Ⓜ M2 Batthyány tér

Porcelánház (5, B5)
This is the shop to source colourful pottery from Hódmezővásárhely in south-eastern Hungary, a centre of that craft for hundreds of years.
☎ 266 3165 ✉ V Váci utca 45 🕑 10am-6pm Mon-Fri, 10am-3pm Sat Ⓜ M3 Ferenciek tere

Zsolnay (5, A4)
For both contemporary and traditional fine eosin porcelain from Pécs, check out this place.
☎ 266 6305 ✉ V Váci utca 19-21 🕑 10am-7pm Ⓜ M3 Ferenciek tere

FOLK ART & SOUVENIRS

Folkart Centrum (5, B5)
Also called 'Népművészet', Folkart is a large shop where everything Magyar-made is available – folk costumes, dolls, painted eggs, embroidered tablecloths – and prices are clearly labelled. The staff are helpful. Similar but even bigger is the Folkart Kézművesház (Folkart Artisan House; 5, A4 ☎ 318 5143; V Régi posta utca 12) further north on the same street.
☎ 318 5840 ✉ V Váci utca 58 🕙 10am-7pm 🚊 15 🚊 47, 49

Holló Atelier (5, B4)
Off the northern end of Váci utca, this place has attractive folk art with a modern look, and remains a personal favourite for buying gifts.
☎ 317 8103 ✉ V Vitkovics Mihály utca 12 🕙 10am-6pm Mon-Fri, 10am-noon Sat Ⓜ M1/2/3 Deák Ferenc tér

Hungaricum (4, B4)
This shop, conveniently located on Castle Hill, sells quality Hungarian handicrafts as well as foodstuffs (eg potted goose liver and honey), wines and brandies.
☎ 487 7306 ✉ I Fortuna utca 1 🕙 9am-9pm 🚊 16 or Várbusz

Intuita (5, B5)
You're not likely to find painted eggs and *pálinka* (brandy) at this gift shop, but it does stock handmade glass, ceramics, bound books etc that are all modern versions of traditional Hungarian crafts.
☎ 266 5864 ✉ V Váci utca 67 🕙 11am-6pm Mon-Fri, 10am-2pm Sat 🚊 15

Játékszerek Anno (5, B2)
The wonderful little 'Anno Playthings' toyshop near Nyugati train station sells finely made reproductions of antique wind-up and other old-fashioned toys.
☎ 302 6234 ✉ VI Teréz körút 54 🕙 10am-6pm Mon-Fri, 9am-1pm Sat Ⓜ M3 Nyugati pályaudvar

FOOD & DRINK

Budapest Wine Society (4, A3)
This society for serious oenophiles has several branches, including one on trendy IX Ráday utca (5, B5; ☎ 219 5647; IX Ráday utca 7). No one knows Hungarian wines like these guys do. There are free tastings on Saturday afternoon.
☎ 212 2569 🖳 www. bortarsasag.hu ✉ I Batthyány utca 59 🕙 10am-8pm Mon-Fri, 10am-6pm Sat Ⓜ M2 Moszkva tér

House of Hungarian Wines (4, B4)
As much a popular tourist attraction as it is a shop, this wine centre offers a crash course in Hungarian viticulture in the heart of the Castle District, but with over 700 wines on display from Hungary's 22 wine regions, and up to 50 wines to try. ☎ 212 1030, 212 1031 🖳 www.winehouse. hu ✉ I Szentháromság tér 6 🕙 noon-8pm 🚊 16 or Várbusz

HUNGARIAN WINE 101

Hungarian wine has undergone something of a renaissance over the last 15 years, and now wineries such as Tiffán, Bock, Szeremley, Thummerer and Szepsy produce very fine wines. Hungary now counts 22 distinct wine-growing areas in Transdanubia, the Balaton region, the Northern Uplands and the Great Plain. The most distinctive reds come from Villány and Szekszárd in southern Transdanubia, the best whites from Somló and around Lake Balaton; and the reds from Eger and sweet whites from Tokaj are well known abroad.

Look for the words *minőségi bor* (quality wine) or *különleges minőségű bor* (premium quality wine), Hungary's version of the French *appellation d'origine controlée*. The first word of the name on a wine bottle indicates where the wine comes from; the second word is the grape variety (eg Villányi Kékfrankos) or the type or brand of wine (eg Tokaji Aszú, Szekszárdi Bikavér). Other important words include *édes* (sweet), *fehér* (white), *félédes* (semisweet), *félszáraz* (semidry or medium), *pezsgő* (sparkling), *száraz* (dry) and *vörös* (red).

Take your pick from many varieties at the Magyar Pálinka Ház

La Boutique des Vins
(5, A3)
Owned and operated by the former sommelier at the exclusive Gundel restaurant, 'The Wine Shop' has an excellent selection of Hungarian wines. Ask the staff to recommend a bottle.
☎ 317 5919 🖳 www.malatinszky.hu 🖂 V József Attila utca 12 ⏱ 10am-6pm Mon-Fri, 10am-3pm Sat
Ⓜ M1/2/3 Deák Ferenc tér

Lekvárium
(5, C4)
This little speciality shop stocks homemade jams and bottled fruit and honey, wine from the Siklós and Villány regions of southern Hungary and fruit-flavoured brandies. It is *the* place to visit to pick up a jar or two of Hungary's greatest edible contribution to humanity – traditionally made *lekvár* (fruit jam), especially the apricot variety.
☎ 321 6543 🖂 VII Dohány utca 39 ⏱ 10am-6pm Mon-Fri, 10am-2pm Sat
Ⓜ M2 Blaha Lujza tér

Magyar Pálinka Ház
(5, C4)
If you're into Hungarian *pálinka*, the exquisite brandy flavoured with everything from peach and plum to cherry, make a beeline for this place.

☎ 338 4219 🖳 www.magyarpalinkahaza.hu 🖂 VIII Rákóczi út 17 ⏱ 9am-7pm Mon-Sat Ⓜ M2 Astoria

Szamos Marcipán
(5, B4)
This shop sells many kinds of marzipan, in every shape and size imaginable. Its ice cream is another major draw.
☎ 317 3643 🖂 V Párizsi utca 3 ⏱ 10am-7pm
Ⓜ M3 Ferenciek tere

ART & ANTIQUES

Anna Antikvitás
(5, A2)
Anna is the place to go if you're in the market for embroidered antique tablecloths and bedlinen.
☎ 302 5461 🖂 V Falk Miksa utca 18-20 🚋 4, 6

Arten Stúdió
(5, B4)
This fine-art gallery is somewhat commercial, with lots of bric-a-brac, but also shows works by such modern Hungarian artists as Árpád Müller and Endre Szász. Enter from Pesti Barnabás utca.
☎ 266 3127 🖂 V Váci utca 25 ⏱ 10am-6.30pm Mon-Fri, 10am-6pm Sat Ⓜ M3 Ferenciek tere

BÁV
(5, A2)
This chain of pawn and secondhand shops, with a number of branches around town, is always a fun place to comb for trinkets and treasures; check out this branch for chinaware, textiles and artwork. Other stores include the VI Andrássy út branch (5, B3; ☎ 342 9143; VI Andrássy út 43) for old jewellery, watches and silver; the V Bécsi utca branch (5, B4; ☎ 318 4403; V Bécsi utca 1-3) for knick-knacks, porcelain and glassware; and the II Margit körút branch (4, C2; ☎ 315 0417; II Margit körút 4) for furniture, lamps and fine porcelain.
☎ 325 2600, 473 0666 🖳 www.bav.hu 🖂 XIII Szent István körút 3

🕙 10am-6pm Mon-Fri, 9am-1pm Sat 🚆 4, 6

Belvárosi Aukciósház
(5, B5)
The 'Inner Town Auction House' usually has themed auctions (jewellery, artwork and graphics, furniture and carpets etc) at 5pm on Monday from September to June, but is open for viewing throughout the week.
☎ 267 3539 ✉ V Váci utca 36 🕙 10am-6pm Mon-Fri, 10am-4pm Sat Ⓜ M3 Ferenciek tere

Kieselbach Galéria
(5, A2)
This is without a doubt the best source in the city for Hungarian painting and other works of fine art, and there are frequent auctions.
☎ 269 3148 🖥 www. kieselbach.hu ✉ V Szent István körút 5 🕙 10am-6pm Mon-Sat 🚆 4, 6

Pintér Antik
(5, A2)
With a positively enormous antique showroom measuring 1800 sq metres in a series of cellars near Parliament, Pintér has everything from furniture and chandeliers to oil paintings and china.
☎ 311 3030 🖥 www. pinterantik.hu ✉ V Falk Miksa utca 10 🕙 10am-6pm Mon-Fri, 10am-2pm Sat 🚆 4, 6

Timpanon
(3, A3)
This seldom-noticed shop in Óbuda sells antique Hungarian folk art of every shape and size: mangle boards, woodcarvings, chests etc. But don't expect any bargains. An early

Browse through the antique-filled cellars of Pintér Antik

19th-century *tulipán láda* (trousseau chest with tulips painted on it) from the Felvidék area of Slovakia will cost you around 130,000Ft. There's a Buda branch called Almárium (4, B5; ☎ 250 5547; I Attila utca 65).
☎ 250 5547 ✉ III Nagyszombat utca 3 🕙 10am-6pm Mon-Fri 🚋 HÉV Tímár utc

BOOKS & MUSIC

Bestsellers
(5, A3)
Still top of the pops for English-language book-shops in Budapest, Bestsellers has novels, travel guides and lots of Hungarica, as well as a large selection of magazines and newspapers.
☎ 312 1295 ✉ V Október 6 utca 11 🕙 9am-6.30pm Mon-Fri, 10am-5pm Sat, 10am-4pm Sun Ⓜ M1/2/3 Deák Ferenc tér

Concerto Hanglemezbolt
(5, C3)
For classical CDs, tapes and vinyl, try the wonderful 'Concerto Record Shop', which is always full of hard-to-find treasures.

☎ 268 9631 ✉ VII Dob utca 33 🕙 noon-7pm Mon-Fri, noon-4pm Sun Ⓜ M2 Astoria

Írók Boltja
(5, B3)
For Hungarian authors in translation, including many of those mentioned on p81, this is the place to go. Writers' Bookshop ☎ 322 1645 ✉ VI Andrássy út 45 Ⓜ M1 Oktogon 🚆 4, 6

Kódex
(5, A2)
At Kódex you'll find Hungarian books on the ground floor and foreign books on the 1st floor, along with a decent selection of classical and jazz CDs.
☎ 428 1010 ✉ V Honvéd utca 5 🕙 9am-6pm Mon-Fri Ⓜ M2 Kossuth Lajos tér

Központi Antikvárium
(5, B4)
For antique and secondhand books in Hungarian, German and English, try the 'Central Antiquarian Bookshop', established in 1885 and the largest of its kind in Budapest.
☎ 317 3514 ✉ V Múzeum körút 13-15 🕙 10am-6.30pm Mon-Fri, 10am-2pm Sat Ⓜ M2 Astoria

READING BUDAPEST
- *Under the Frog* (Tibor Fischer, 2001)
- *Homage to the Eighth District* (Giorgio and Nicola Pressburger, 1990)
- *Liquidation* (Imre Kertész, 2003)
- *Memoir of Hungary: 1944–1948* (Sándor Márai, 2001)
- *Prague* (Arthur Phillips, 2002)

Libri Könyvpalota (5, C4)
Spread over two floors, the huge 'Book Palace' has a selection of English-language novels, art books, guidebooks, maps and music, and a café and internet access on the 1st floor. For books in English and other languages specifically on Hungarian subjects, a more useful branch is Libri Stúdium (5, B4; ☎ 318 5680; V Váci utca 22).
☎ 267 4844 ✉ VII Rákóczi út 12 ☽ 10am-7.30pm Mon-Fri, 10am-3pm Sat Ⓜ M2 Astoria

Pendragon (5, A1)
While this 'English bookshop', which takes its name from the legend of King Arthur, has an excellent selection of English books and guides (including Lonely Planet titles), most Anglophones will have a hard time making themselves understood here.
☎ 340 4426 ✉ XIII Pozsonyi út 21-23 ☽ 10am-6pm Mon-Fri, 10am-2pm Sat 🚌 4, 6

Red Bus Secondhand Bookstore (5, B4)
Below the popular hostel of that name is the top shop in town for used (as opposed to antiquarian) English-language books.
☎ 337 7453 ✉ V Sem-melweis utca 14 🖥 www.redbusbudapest.hu ☽ 11am-6pm Mon-Fri, 10am-2pm Sat Ⓜ M2 Astoria

Rózsavölgyi (5, B4)
This music shop is a good choice for CDs and tapes of traditional folk music.
☎ 318 3312 ✉ V Szervita tér 5 ☽ 9.30am-7pm Mon, Tue, Thu & Fri, 10am-7pm Wed, 10am-5pm Sat Ⓜ M1/2/3 Deák Ferenc tér

Szőnyi Antikváriuma (5, A2)
This long-established antiquarian bookshop has an excellent selection of antique prints and maps (look in the drawers) as well as books.
☎ 311 6431 🖥 www.szonyi.hu ✉ V Szent Istvánkörút 3 ☽ 10am-6pm Mon-Fri, 9am-1pm Sat 🚌 4, 6

FASHION & CLOTHING

Balogh Kesztyű (5, B4)
If he can have a pair of bespoke shoes (Vass, opposite), why can't she have a pair of custom-made gloves? You'll get them here at 'Balogh Gloves' – and in any number of materials.
☎ 266 1942 ✉ V Haris köz 2 ☽ 10am-6pm Mon-Fri, 10.30am-1pm Sat Ⓜ M3 Ferenciek tere

Ciánkáli (5, D3)
Whatever your 'drag' of choice happens to be – 1960s camp to leather or military – the folks at this antifashion emporium of used and vintage clothes will have you kitted out before you know it.
☎ 341 0540 🖥 www.majomketrec.hu ✉ VII Dohány utca 94 ☽ 10am-7pm Mon-Fri, 10am-2pm Sat 🚎 trolleybus 74

Old books for sale in Szőnyi Antikváriuma

TOP FIVE CDS

- *The Prisoner's Song* – Muzsikás with Márta Sebestyén
- *Romano Trip: Gypsy Grooves from Eastern Europe* – Romano Drom
- *Lechajem Rebbe* – the Budapest Klezmer Band
- *Hungarian Astronaut* – Anima Sound System
- *With the Gypsy Violin Around the World* – Sándor Déki Lakatos and his Gypsy Band

Iguana (5, C5)
This shop sells vintage leather, suede and velvet pieces from the 1950s, 1960s and 1970s, as well as its own trousers, skirts, shirts and blouses. There's a district IX branch (5, C6; ☎ 215 3475; IX Tompa utca 1).
☎ 317 1627 ⊠ VIII Krúdy utca 9 ☽ 10am-7pm Mon-Fri, 10am-2pm Sat 🚊 4, 6

Monarchia (5, B4)
This fashion house stocks funky one-off and made-to-measure items that have a distinctly Magyar stamp. There is a branch in the West End City Centre (5, B2; ☎ 238 7172).
☎ 318 3146 ⊠ V Szabadsajtó út 6 Ⓜ M3 Ferenciek tere

Náray Tamás (5, B4)
The principal outlet for Hungary's most celebrated and controversial designer, the Paris-trained Tamás Náray, stocks elegant ready-to-wear fashion and accessories for women, and also accepts tailoring orders.
☎ 266 2473 ⊠ V Károlyi Mihály utca 12 ☽ noon-8pm Mon-Fri, 10am-2pm Sat Ⓜ M3 Ferenciek tere

Vass (5, B4)
A traditional shoemaker that stocks both ready-made and bespoke footwear, Vass has a reputation that goes back to 1896, and some people travel to Hungary just to have their shoes made here.
☎ 318 2375 💻 www.

vass-shoes.hu ⊠ V Haris köz 2 ☽ 10am-6pm Mon-Fri, 10am-2pm Sat Ⓜ M3 Ferenciek tere

HOUSEHOLD GOODS

Magma (5, B4)
In the centre of the Belváros, this showroom focuses on Hungarian design and designers – with everything from glassware and porcelain to textiles and furniture.
☎ 235 0277 ⊠ V Petőfi Sándor utca 11 ☽ 10am-5pm Mon-Fri, 10am-3pm Sat Ⓜ M3 Ferenciek tere

Nádortex (5, A4)
Goose-feather or down products such as pillows (from 12,000Ft) or duvets (comforters; from 22,000Ft) are of excellent quality in Hungary and a highly recommended purchase. Nádortex, small but reliable, has some of the best prices.
☎ 317 0030 ⊠ V József nádor tér 12 ☽ 10am-6pm Mon-Fri Ⓜ M1 Vörösmarty tér

CLOTHING & SHOE SIZES

Women's Clothing

Aust/UK	8	10	12	14	16	18
Europe	36	38	40	42	44	46
Japan	5	7	9	11	13	15
USA	6	8	10	12	14	16

Women's Shoes

Aust/USA	5	6	7	8	9	10
Europe	35	36	37	38	39	40
France only	35	36	38	39	40	42
Japan	22	23	24	25	26	27
UK	3½	4½	5½	6½	7½	8½

Men's Clothing

Aust	92	96	100	104	108	112
Europe	46	48	50	52	54	56

Japan	S	M	M		L	
UK/USA	35	36	37	38	39	40

Men's Shirts (Collar Sizes)

Aust/Japan	38	39	40	41	42	43
Europe	38	39	40	41	42	43
UK/USA	15	15½	16	16½	17	17½

Men's Shoes

Aust/UK	7	8	9	10	11	12
Europe	41	42	43	44½	46	47
Japan	26	27	27.5	28	29	30
USA	7½	8½	9½	10½	11½	12½

Measurements approximate only; try before you buy.

Eating

Budapest is currently undergoing something of a restaurant revolution. Stodgy and heavy Hungarian food is being 'enlightened' and rechristened as *kortárs magyar konyha* (modern Hungarian cuisine) at many restaurants. At the same time, more vegetarian restaurants have opened up in recent years, and ethnic food – from Middle Eastern and Greek to takeaway Thai and Chinese – has become very popular. It makes a nice change from the not-so-distant days when to eat out most often meant tussling with an overcooked *bécsiszelet* (Wiener schnitzel) in yet another smoky *vendéglő* (small restaurant).

The day's eating starts for most Hungarians – generally not big eaters of *reggeli* (breakfast) – with a cup of tea or coffee and a plain bread roll at the kitchen table or on the way to work. *Ebéd* (lunch), eaten at around 1pm, is the main meal of the day, and might consist of two or three courses – most restaurants offer a good-value lunch *menü* (set menu). *Vacsora* (dinner or supper), when eaten at home, is often just sliced meat, cheese and some pickled vegetables.

An *étterem* is a restaurant with a wide-ranging menu, sometimes including international dishes. A *vendéglő* or *kisvendéglő* is smaller, and is supposed to serve inexpensive regional dishes or home cooking;

A traditional restaurant sign

however the name tends to be used somewhat indiscriminately. An *étkezde* is something like a *vendéglő* but cheaper and smaller, not unlike the British 'caff'. The term *csárda* originally signified a country inn with a rustic atmosphere, Gypsy music and hearty local dishes – now it seems to be any place that hangs up a couple of painted plates and a few strands of dried paprika. A *bisztró* is a much cheaper sit-down place that is often *önkiszolgáló* (self-service). Traditional coffee houses and newly popular teahouses are primarily known for their teas and coffees, but sometimes serve cakes and light meals as well.

Most restaurants are open from 10am or 11am to 11pm or midnight.

BUDA

Buda can't match Pest for quantity, but it does have high-quality, very atmospheric dining venues.

Castle Hill

Café Pierrot (4, B4)
Hungarian, International €€€
This very stylish and long-established café-cum-bar-cum-restaurant is one of the very few recommendable places on Castle Hill. The décor is, well, clownish and there's live piano music nightly. The food is Hungaro-hybrid and quite good, and staff are exceptionally friendly.
☎ 375 6971 ⊠ I Fortuna utca 14 🕑 11am-midnight 🚌 16

Rivalda (4, C4)
International €€€
An international café restaurant in an old convent with some modern Hungarian favourites, Rivalda has a thespian theme and a delightful garden courtyard. The menu changes frequently, and the wine list is among the best around.
☎ 489 0236 ⊠ I Színház utca 5–9 🕑 11.30am-11.30pm 🚌 16

Gellért Hill & the Tabán

Aranyszarvas (4, C6)
Hungarian €€€
Set in an 18th-century inn literally at the foot of Castle Hill, the 'Golden Stag' serves up mainly game dishes. There's evening piano music from Thursday to Saturday, and the covered outside terrace in summer, when grills are available, is inviting. Vegetarians should give this place a wide berth and head for nearby Éden.
☎ 375 6451 ⊠ I Szarvas tér 1 🕑 noon-11pm 🚌 86

Éden (4, C6)
Vegetarian €
This place in a mid-18th-century townhouse below Castle Hill must have the classiest location of any vegetarian restaurant anywhere. Seating is in the 1st-floor dining room and, in warmer months, in the pleasant courtyard.
☎ 375 7575 ⊠ I Döbrentei utca 9 🕑 noon-11pm Sun-Thu 🚌 86

Marcello (5, A6)
Italian €€
Popular with students from the nearby university since it was founded some 15 years ago, this father-and-son-owned operation offers reliable Italian fare at affordable prices. The lasagne is almost legendary in these parts.
☎ 466 6231 ⊠ XI Bartók Béla út 40 🕑 noon-10pm Mon-Sat 🚋 49

TIPPING ETIQUETTE

Never leave money on the table – this is considered rude – but tell the waiter how much you're paying in total. If the bill is, say, 2700Ft, you're paying with a 5000Ft note and you think the waiter deserves around 10%, first ask if service is included (some restaurants add it to the bill automatically). If it isn't, say you're paying 3000Ft or that you want 2000Ft back.

It is not unknown for waiters to try to rip off foreigners. They may try to bring you an unordered dish or make a 'mistake' when tallying the bill. If you think there's a discrepancy, ask for the menu and check the bill carefully. If you've been taken for more than 15% or 20% of the bill, call for the manager. Otherwise just don't leave a tip.

Golden stags watch over diners in the Aranyszarvas

Tabáni Terasz (4, C6)
Hungarian €€
This charming terrace restaurant at the foot of Castle Hill is giving the long-established Aranyszarvas (p47) a run for its money. It's a modern take on the theme, with less calorific Hungarian dishes and an excellent wine selection. The candle-lit cellar is a delight in winter.
☎ 201 1086 ✉ I Apród utca 10 🕑 11.30am-midnight 🚌 86

Víziváros
Kacsa (4, C2)
Hungarian €€€
'Duck' is the place to go for, well, duck. It's a fairly elegant place, with art on the walls and piano music in the evening, so dress appropriately. Fresh ingredients, formal service and pricey wines.
☎ 201 9992 ✉ II Fő utca 75 🕑 noon-midnight 🚌 86

Le Jardin de Paris (4, C4)
French €€€
'The Parisian Garden' is housed in Kapisztory House, a wonderful old townhouse abutting an ancient castle wall. The back garden ablaze in fairy lights is enchanting in summer. Try the homemade pâtés and the brasserie-style steak and chips.
☎ 201 0047 ✉ II Fő utca 20 🕑 noon-midnight 🚌 86

Malomtó (4, B1)
Hungarian, International €€€
The 'Mill Lake' has up-to-date, fresh décor and an inspired menu of modern dishes – especially game and seafood – many with an Asian spin. But its major draw is its unique position on the edge of a tiny lake; a seat on the terrace in the warmer months is not just recommended, it's mandatory.
☎ 336 1830 ✉ II Frankel Leó utca 48 🕑 noon-10pm 🚃 17

Maros Söröző (4, A4)
Slovakian €€
This brasserie serves some of the best (and most generous) Slovakian dishes in town. Try the *sztrapacska* (potato dumplings) with smoked ham, or the beef in red wine with noodles, which, of course, must be washed down with Zlatý Bažant draught beer.
☎ 212 3746 ✉ XII Maros utca 16 🕑 11am-11pm 🚃 61

Marxim (4, A2)
Italian €
A short walk from Moszkva tér, this odd place is a hangout for teens who have added a layer of their own graffiti to the communist memorabilia and kitsch. We all know Stalin *szuksz*, but it's a curiosity for those who might appreciate the Lenin and Red October pizzas and the campy Stalinist décor.
☎ 316 0231 ✉ II Kis Rókus utca 23 🕑 noon-1am Mon-Thu, noon-2am Fri & Sat, 6pm-1am Sun Ⓜ M2 Moszkva tér

Szent Jupát (4, A3)
Hungarian, Late Night €
Szent Jupát is the classic late-night choice for solid Hungarian fare – consider splitting a dish with a friend. It's within easy striking distance of both Buda and Pest.
☎ 212 2923 ✉ II Retek utca 16 🕑 noon-6am Ⓜ M2 Moszkva tér

Új Lanzhou (4, C3)
Chinese €€
They say that the 'New Lanzhou' is not as authentic as its minuscule sister restaurant Lanzhou (5, D4; ☎ 314 1080; VIII Luther utca) over in Pest, but you could have fooled me. This place is also more stylish, so no doubt it will be a winner.
☎ 201 9247 ✉ II Fő utca 71 🕑 11.30am-11pm 🚌 86

A chalkboard menu

PEST

Pest-side eateries are often more relaxed and (it must be said) hipper than in Buda.

Inner Town

Falafel Faloda (6, B3)
Vegetarian, Israeli €

This inexpensive place just down from Budapest's theatre district has Israeli-style nosh. You pay a fixed price to stuff a piece of pitta bread with, or fill a plastic container from, a great assortment of salads. It also has a good variety of soups.
☎ 267 9567 ✉ VI Paulay Ede utca 53 🕐 10am-8pm Mon-Fri, 10am-6pm Sat 🚎 trolleybus 70, 78

Fatál (6, B5)
Hungarian €€

This place serves massive Hungarian meals on *fatál* (wooden platters), or in iron cauldrons, in three rustic rooms. And follow the rules: bring your appetite and friends; avoid the noisy back room; and book in advance.
☎ 266 2607 ✉ V Váci utca 67 🕐 11.30am-2am 🚎 47, 49

Károlyi Étterem (6, B5)
Hungarian €€

This place beckons not so much for the food (though it is good) but for its location in the renovated Károly Palace, with a wonderful terrace in the palace courtyard open in the warmer months. The menu has lots of options for vegetarians.
☎ 328 0240 ✉ V Károlyi Mihály utca 16 🕐 10am-11pm 🚎 15

Kárpátia (6, B5)
Hungarian €€€

A veritable palace of fin-de-siècle design dating back 120 years, the 'Carpathia' serves almost modern Hungarian and Transylvanian specialities in both its restaurant and cheaper pub, and there is a lovely covered garden terrace. This is the place to hear authentic *csárdás* Gypsy music.
☎ 317 3596 ✉ V Ferenciek tere 7-8 🕐 11am-11pm Ⓜ M3 Ferenciek tere

Képíró (6, B5)
French €€€

Using the old Hungarian word for 'painter', this restaurant is one of the more stylishly appointed eateries in town, with provocative frescoes on the walls and canned jazz. The food is French classical (it gets a red Michelin mention) and the service professional, and there is a decent selection of vegetarian dishes.
☎ 266 0430 ✉ V Képíró utca 3 🕐 noon-3pm & 6pm-midnight Mon-Fri, 6pm-midnight Sat & Sun Ⓜ M3 Kálvin tér

Óceán Bár & Grill (6, A4)
Seafood €€€

This place is making waves with its fresher-than-fresh seafood flown in daily from Scandinavia, and its congenial décor. I'll come back for the curried crabmeat soufflé and the boiled lobster. There's a three-course set lunch for 5000Ft.
☎ 266 1826 ✉ V Petőfi tér 3-5 🕐 noon-midnight 🚎 2, 2A

The Kárpátia offers Hungarian and Transylvanian specialities and traditional live music

Spoon (5, A4)

International €€€

If you like the idea of dining on the high waters but still remaining tethered to the bank, Spoon's for you. It serves international cuisine amid bright and breezy surrounds, and the choices for vegetarians are great. You can't beat the views of the castle and Széchenyi Chain Bridge. It also does sushi and sashimi.

☎ 411 0933 ✉ off V Vigadó tér 🕓 noon–midnight 🚊 2, 2A

Sushi An (6, A4)

Japanese €€

This tiny sushi bar next to the British embassy in central Pest is great for sushi and sashimi, but even better for Japanese sets served with miso soup. There's room to swing a cat in here, but not much more.

A MAGYAR MATCH MADE IN HEAVEN

The pairing of food with wine is as great an obsession here as it is in France. Sweets like strudel go very well indeed with a glass of Tokaji Aszú, but this wine also matches cheeses such as Roquefort, Stilton and Gorgonzola. A bone-dry Olaszrizling from Badacsony is a superb complement to any fish dish, but especially Lake Balaton's pike perch. It would be a shame to 'waste' a big wine like a Vili Papa Cuvée on simple Hungarian dishes like gulyás or pörkölt; try instead Kékfrankos or Szekszárd Kadarka. Cream-based dishes stand up well to late-harvest Furmint, and pork dishes are nice with new Furmint or Kékfrankos. Try Hárslevelű with poultry.

☎ 317 4239 ✉ V Harmincad utca 4 🕓 noon–10pm Ⓜ M1/2/3 Deák Ferenc tér

Taverna Pireus Rembetiko (6, B6)

Greek €€

Overlooking a patch of green and facing the Nagycsarnok (p39), this place serves reasonably priced and pretty authentic Greek fare. Rembetiko is a style of traditional Greek music; there are live performances on Friday and Saturday evening. The courtyard is tempting in summer.

☎ 266 0292 ✉ V Fővám tér 2-3 🕓 noon–midnight 🚊 47, 49

Trattoria Toscana (6, A6)

Italian €€

Hard by the Danube, this trattoria serves rustic and very authentic Italian and Tuscan food, including ribollita alla chiantigiana, a hearty vegetable soup made with cannellini beans and Parmesan cheese.

☎ 327 0045 ✉ V Belgrád rakpart 13 🕓 noon–midnight 🚌 15

Vegetarium (6, B5)

Vegetarian €

A basement restaurant just off Egyetem tér, the Vegetarium, Budapest's (and Hungary's) oldest meat-free restaurant, serves vegetarian and organic food of the old style; there are lots of choices for vegans here too.

☎ 484 0848 ✉ V Cukor utca 3 🕓 11.30am-10pm Mon-Sat Ⓜ M3 Ferenciek tere

Northern Inner Town

Café Kör (6, A3)
International €€
Just behind the Basilica of St Stephen, the 'Circle Café' is a great place for a light meal at any time, including late breakfast. Salads, desserts and daily specials are always recommended, and there are more ambitious three- or four-course wine-tasting menus.
☎ 311 0053 ⊠ V Sas utca 17 🕑 10am-10pm Mon-Sat 🚊 15

Café Mokka (6, A3)
International €€€
The name of the game here is 'ethno-cuisine', with a mishmash of dishes; you'll virtually need a map and compass to read the menu. But I love the space, the wine list and the great African theme.
☎ 328 0081 ⊠ V Sas utca 4 🕑 noon-midnight 🚊 15

Gresham Kávéház (5, A3)
International €€€
Hotel coffee shops don't usually make the grade, but this one in a stunning newly renovated hotel (see p71) is worth its weight in majolica tiles. There's live jazz every Thursday, Friday and Saturday from 7pm.
☎ 268 5110 ⊠ V Roosevelt tér 5-6 🕑 6.30am-11.30pm Mon-Fri, 7am-11.30pm Sat, noon-10pm Sun Ⓜ M1 Vörösmarty tér 🚊 15 🚋 2

Kama Sutra (6, A3)
Indian €€
This new arrival is a welcome one indeed: decent curries and tandoori dishes in upbeat surrounds in the very heart of town. It's a cut

FOR THE LOVE OF PAPRIKA
A spice as Magyar as St Stephen's right hand (p13); paprika is not only used in cooking but it also appears on restaurant tables as a condiment beside the salt and pepper shakers. It's quite a mild spice and is used predominantly with sour cream or in *rántás*, a heavy roux of pork lard and flour added to cooked vegetables. The most famous meat dish that uses paprika is *gulyás* or *gulyásleves*, a thick beef soup cooked with onions, cubed potatoes and paprika, and usually eaten as a main course. *Pörkölt* (stew) is closer to what foreigners call 'goulash'; the addition of sour cream, less paprika and white meat such as chicken makes the dish *paprikás*. *Tokány* is similar to *pörkölt* and *paprikás* except that the meat is cut into strips, there's as much black pepper as paprika, and bacon, sausage or mushroom are added.

above the usual curry-house atmosphere and the perfect place for a meal before moving on for the evening.
☎ 373 0092 ⊠ V Október 6 utca 19 🕑 11am-11pm 🚊 15

Kisharang (6, A3)
Hungarian €
The central 'Little Bell' is an *étkezde* that is on the top of the list with students and staff of the nearby Central European University. The daily specials are something to look forward to, and the retro décor is a bit of fun.
☎ 269 3861 ⊠ V Október 6 utca 17 🕑 11am-8pm Mon-Fri, 11.30am-4.30pm Sat & Sun 🚊 15

La Fontaine (6, A3)
French €€€
'The Fountain' is a Parisian-style café theatre, with a much wider choice of fish dishes than one would normally find in such a restaurant. The relatively simple food is good, especially the leg of lamb and the *steak frites*.
☎ 317 3715 ⊠ V Mérleg utca 10 🕑 noon-2.30pm Mon-Fri, 7-10.30pm daily 🚊 15

Lou Lou (6, A3)
French €€€
One of the most popular places with expatriate *Français* in Budapest is this

bistro with excellent daily specials. Two signature dishes are the marinated grilled breast of duck with orange and Arabica coffee sauce and the rack of lamb with garlic and *haricots verts*.

☎ 312 4505 ✉ V Vigyázó Ferenc utca 4 ✿ noon-3pm & 7-11pm Mon-Fri, 7-11pm Sat 🚌 15

Újlipótváros & Terézváros

Alhambra (6, B2)
Spanish, Moroccan €€
Almost certainly inspired by the celebrated Moro restaurant in London, Alhambra serves Spanish food with a North African twist, as well as straightforward Moroccan dishes such as couscous and tajines.

☎ 354 1068 ✉ VI Jókai tér 3 ✿ noon-midnight Mon-Fri, 6pm-midnight Sat & Sun Ⓜ M1 Oktogon

Articsóka (6, B3)
Mediterranean €€€
The charming 'Artichoke' is tastefully decorated, and has an atrium, rooftop terrace and a theatre that can accommodate 100 people. There's live music every second week of the month, and the atmosphere should win a prize. The food is more Hungaro-Med than Italian, but pasta dishes are especially recommended.

☎ 302 7757 ✉ VI Zichy Jenő utca 17 ✿ 11am-midnight Ⓜ M3 Arany János utca

Firkász (3, B6)
Hungarian €€
Set up by former journalists (the name means 'hack' in Hungarian), Firkász is a retro Hungarian restaurant with lovely old mementos on the walls, excellent

home cooking, a great wine list and an unbeatable location.

☎ 450 1118 ✉ Tátra utca 18 ✿ noon-midnight 🚌 15

Főzelék Faló (6, B3)
Hungarian €
Some people say that this *étkezde*, which keeps relatively extended hours, is the best in town. It's very convenient for the bars of Liszt Ferenc tér, but is always busy, and it seems like there's never a place to sit down.

☎ 266 6398 ✉ VI Nagymező utca 18 ✿ 9am-10pm Mon-Fri, 10am-7pm Sat Ⓜ M1 Opera

Három Testvér (6, C3)
Middle Eastern, Self-Service €
Great any time but especially for a late-night or postclub snack, the 'Three Brothers' have branches throughout Pest, including at Szent István körút (6, A1;

☎ 329 2951; XIII Szent István körút 20-22) and Teréz körút (6, B2;

☎ 312 5835; VI Teréz körút 60-62).

☎ 342 2377 ✉ VII Erzsébet körút 17 ✿ 9-3am 🚃 4, 6

Marquis de Salade (6, B2)
International €€
This is a serious hybrid of a place, with dishes from Russia and Azerbaijan as well as Hungary (and it serves more than just *salade*). There are lots of quality vegetarian choices, too, in this basement restaurant.

☎ 302 4086 ✉ VI Hajós utca 43 ✿ 11-1am 🚃 trolleybus 72, 73

Enjoy simple, excellent food at the popular Menza (opposite)

Menza (6, C3)
Hungarian €€
On Budapest's most lively square, this upmarket Hungarian restaurant takes its name from the Hungarian for a drab school canteen – something it is anything but. Book a table; it's fabulously stylish and always packed by diners who come for the simply but perfectly cooked Hungarian classics with a modern spin.
☎ 413 1482 ✉ VI Liszt Ferenc tér 2 🕑 10am–midnight Ⓜ M1 Oktogon

Móri Kisvendéglő (3, B5)
Hungarian, Jewish €
Sample some of the best home-cooked Hungarian Jewish food in Budapest at this simple *borozó* (wine bar) and *étkezde*. But, as the owner would like to warn our 'dear readers', get here by 3pm if you want to eat the famous *főzelék*.
☎ 349 8390 ✉ XIII Pozsonyi út 39 🕑 10am–8pm Mon-Thu, 10am-3pm Fri. 🚋 trolleybus 76, 79

Mosselen (6, A1)
Belgian €€
This pleasant gastropub serves Belgian (and some Hungarian) specialities, including its namesake, mussels, and has a wide selection of Belgian beers, including some of the fruit-flavoured ones; a tasting of six beers costs 1650Ft.
☎ 452 0535 🖳 www.mosselen.hu ✉ XIII Pannónia utca 14 🕑 noon–midnight 🚌 15

Pesti Vendéglő (6, B4)
Hungarian €€
Here is a great choice for someone trying traditional Hungarian specialities for the first time. This very popular family-run and clean eatery offers a lighter take on standard Hungarian favourites, and the staff are very welcoming and helpful.
☎ 266 3227 ✉ VI Paulay Ede utca 5 🕑 11am-11pm Ⓜ M1/2/3 Deák Ferenc tér

Pozsonyi Kisvendéglő (3, B6)
Hungarian €
Visit this neighbourhood restaurant offering the ultimate local experience: gargantuan portions of standard Hungarian favourites, rock-bottom prices and a cast of local characters. There's a bank of tables on the pavement in summer.
☎ 329 2911 ✉ XIII Radnóti Miklós utca 38 🕑 11am-midnight 🚋 trolleybus 76, 79

Troféa Grill (5, B1)
International, Buffet €€
When you really could eat a horse, head for the Troféa – there must be one there somewhere. It's an enormous buffet of more than 100 cold and hot dishes over which diners swarm like bees.

DO IT YOURSELF
Budapest is a self-caterer's heaven, with some 20 large food markets. Most of them are in Pest, and usually open from around 6am to 6pm on weekdays, and to 2pm on Saturday. The **Nagycsarnok** (p39) is the biggest; head here for fruit and vegetables, deli items, fish and meat. If you've got the urge for something sweet, **Mézes Kuckó** (3, B6; XIII Jászai Mari tér 4; 🕑 10am-6pm Mon-Fri, 9am-1pm Sat Oct-May) has nut-and-honey cookies to die for, and their colourful gingerbread hearts make excellent gifts. Budapest's best cheese shop, **Nagy Tamás** (6, B4; ☎ 317 4268; V Gerlóczy utca 3; 🕑 9am-6pm Mon-Fri, 9am-1pm Sat) stocks more than 200 varieties of Hungarian and imported cheeses, **Butterfly** (6, C2; VI Teréz körút 20; 🕑 10am-7pm Mon-Fri, 10am-2pm Sat) is *the* place in Pest for ice cream, as you'll be able to deduce from the queues outside.

Considering there's goose liver and salmon on the table (at least for a while), it's good value.
☎ 270 0366 ✉ XIII Visegrádi utca 50/a ⏰ noon-midnight Mon-Fri, 11.30am-midnight Sat, 11.30am-9pm Sun Ⓜ M3 Lehel tér

Vogue (3, B5)
South Slav €€€
This fine old vessel moored off XIII Szent István Park has fine views south to Margaret Bridge and the Széchenyi Chain Bridge. Unusually, you can take in both sides of the river. The food is Serbian and other South Slav – *čevapčiči* (spicy meatballs), *pljeskavica* (spicy meat patties) and *ražnjiči* (shish kebab) – always grilled and always in large portions.
☎ 350 7000, 06 30 942 5027 ✉ XIII Újpesti alsó rakpart 1 ⏰ 11-1am 🚎 trolleybus 76, 79

Erzsébetváros
Al-Amir (6, B3)
Middle Eastern €€
Arguably the most authentic Middle Eastern (in this case, Syrian) place in town. Al-Amir also has a window selling great-quality takeaway kebabs and falafel
☎ 352 1422 ✉ VII Király utca 17 ⏰ noon-11pm Ⓜ M1 Bajcsy-Zsilinszky út

Carmel Pince (6, C4)
Jewish €€
Decidedly *not* kosher – signs outside will warn you of that fact in six living languages – but the 'Carmel Cellar' has authentic Ashkenazi specialities such as gefilte fish, matzo-ball soup and a

cholent almost as good as the one Aunt Goldie used to make. There's live *klezmer* music (see p65) on Thursday evening, and a good-value three-course tourist menu.
☎ 322 1834, 342 4585 ✉ VII Kazinczy utca 31 ⏰ noon-11pm 🚎 trolleybus 74

Fausto (6, B4)
Italian €€€€
Still the most upmarket Italian restaurant – and one of the most pleasant dining experiences – in town, Fausto has brilliant pasta dishes, daily specials and desserts. The Italian wine selection is huge, and there are lots of choices for vegetarians.
☎ 269 6806 ✉ VII Dohány utca 5 ⏰ noon-3pm & 7pm-11pm Mon-Sat 🚎 trolleybus 74

Kinor David (6, B4)
Kosher €€
Budapest's largest kosher restaurant, 'David's Harp', is a cut above the usual and serves dinner, as well as special fish dishes and Israeli treats. Pay in advance for Sabbath meals (Friday dinner and Saturday lunch).
☎ 512 8783 ✉ VII Dohány utca 10 ⏰ 11am-11pm Mon-Fri & Sun, noon-2pm Sat 🚎 trolleybus 74

Magdalena Merlo (6, C3)
Hungarian, Italian €€
This restaurant serves an odd mix of Hungarian and Italian dishes. What's more, since it was the 'Svejk' (from Jaroslav Hašek's satirical novel *The Good Soldier Schweik*) for many years, it has retained a page of nostalgic Czech and

Slovak dishes for those who can't let go of the memories.
☎ 322 3278 ✉ VII Király utca 59 ⏰ 10am-midnight 🚎 4, 6

Spinoza Café (6, B4)
International €€
This very attractive café restaurant in the Jewish district has become a personal favourite both for meals and as a chill-out zone. The food is an unusual (but successful) hybrid of Hungarian, Dutch and Jewish; try the signature chicken with honey and garlic or the roast goose leg with apple and red cabbage. The venue includes both an art gallery and theatre, and there's live music on Thursday from 7pm.
☎ 413 7488 ✉ VII Dob utca 15 ⏰ 11am-11pm 🚎 47, 49

Józsefváros & Ferencváros
BioPont (6, C5)
Vegetarian €
In the Darshan Udvar complex (p59), this is a pleasant place for a meatless organic meal, with all dishes available in both full and half portions. There are also 'bio' sandwiches and pizzas.
☎ 266 4601 ✉ VIII Krúdy utca 7 ⏰ 10am-10pm Mon-Fri, noon-10pm Sat & Sun 🚎 4, 6

Fülemüle (6, C5)
Hungarian, Jewish €€
This quaint Hungarian restaurant that looks like time stood still just before WWII is quite a find in deepest Józsefváros and well worth the search. Dishes mingle Hungarian

and international tastes with some old-style Jewish favourites.

☎ 266 7947 ⊠ VIII Kőfaragó utca 5 🕑 noon-11pm 🚊 7

Múzeum (6, C5)
Hungarian €€€
Come here if you want to really dine in style. Múzeum is a café- restaurant that is still going strong after more than a century at the same location near the National Museum. The food is excellent and reliable, if not particularly inventive, and there is a good-value, three-course lunch set menu.

☎ 338 4221, 267 0375 ⊠ VIII Múzeum körút 12 🕑 noon-midnight Mon-Sat 🚊 47, 49

Pata Negra (6, B5)
Spanish €€
The 'Black Foot' – it's a special kind of Spanish cured ham – is a cellar-like Spanish tapas bar and restaurant just off trendy Ráday utca. There are good cheese and excellent wine selections, and it's very vegetarian-friendly.

☎ 215 5616 ⊠ IX Kálvin tér 8 🕑 11am-midnight Mon-Wed, 11-1am Thu & Fri, noon-1am Sat, noon-midnight Sun Ⓜ M3 Kálvin tér

Pink Cadillac (6, C6)
Italian €
More of an upbeat 1950s diner than a pizzeria, the Pink Cadillac still reigns supreme on Ráday utca after all this time. If you don't like the surrounds, base yourself in the Paris Texas cocktail

Spinoza Café (opposite), where food, art and music meet

bar next door and have your pizza delivered.

☎ 216 1412 ⊠ IX Ráday utca 22 🕑 11-12.30am Sun-Thu, 11-1am Fri & Sat 🚊 15

Soul Café (6, B6)
International €€
One of the better choices along a street full of so-so restaurants and cafés, the Soul has inventive Continental food and décor. You can order anything from a sandwich or pizza to a full meal, including many vegetarian options. It has a great terrace.

☎ 217 6986 ⊠ IX Ráday utca 11-13 🕑 noon-1am Ⓜ M3 Kálvin tér

Stex Alfred (6, C5)
Hungarian, Late Night €€
A big, noisy place that's open almost 24 hours, the Stex offers soups, sandwiches, pasta, fish and meat dishes, as well as vegetarian choices and, best of all, breakfast. It transforms into a lively bar late at night.

☎ 318 5716 ⊠ VIII József körút 55-57 🕑 8-6am Ⓜ M3 Ferenc körút

Vörös Postakocsi (6, C6)
Hungarian €€
What was for over three decades a forgettable eatery serving Hungarian stodge has reemerged Phoenix-like as a trendy retro-Hungarian restaurant. To see how modern Hungarians think they used to eat when times were tougher (and less health-conscious), visit the 'Red Postal Coach'.

☎ 217 6756 ⊠ IX Ráday utca 15 🕑 11.30am-midnight 🚊 15

Andrássy út
Goa (6, B3)
International €€€
This new, well-dressed kid on the block is currently *the* place to be seen to be. And the food's worth going for too; the salads are especially recommended.

☎ 302 2570 ⊠ VI Andrássy út 8 🕑 noon-midnight Ⓜ M1 Bajcsy-Zsilinszky út

Napfényes Ízek (6, D2)
Vegetarian €
'Sunny Tastes' is a bit out of the way unless you're staying near Andrássy út, but

the wholesome foods and speciality cakes are worth the trip. There is an organic shop where you can stock up on both packaged and baked goods, including excellent cakes.
☎ 351 5649 ✉ VII Rózsa utca 39 ⏰ 10am-11pm Mon-Fri, noon-10.30pm Sat & Sun. 🚋 trolleybus 73, 76

Vörös és Fehér (6, B3)
Hungarian €€€
The 'Red and White' is all about wine – Hungarian to be precise – and here you can order from the top of the shelf by the 0.1L to sip and compare. The menu is brief, but has come into its own in recent years; the pork

The fashionable Goa restaurant in the heart of Pest

dishes are superb.
☎ 413 1545 ✉ VI Andrássy út 41 ⏰ 11am-midnight Ⓜ M1 Oktogon

City Park

Bagolyvár (5, D1)
Hungarian €€
With reworked Hungarian classics that make it a winner, the 'Owl's Castle' attracts the Budapest cognoscenti, who leave its sister restaurant next door, Gundel, to the expense-account brigade. It's staffed entirely by women – in the kitchen, at tables and in front of house.
☎ 468 3110 ✉ XIV Állatkerti út 2 ⏰ noon-11pm Ⓜ M1 Hősök tere

Robinson (5, D1)
International €€€
Inside the leafy City Park, Robinson is the place to secure a table on the lakeside terrace on a warm summer's evening. There are excellent starters like sliced goose liver and homemade venison pâté to begin the dining experience. Mains include *fogas* (Balaton pike perch), grilled tuna and smoked duck breast.
☎ 422 0222 ✉ XIV Városligeti tó ⏰ noon-4pm & 6pm-midnight Ⓜ M1 Hősök tere

MEALS WITH A VIEW

Views from on high are rather thin on the ground in a city of baroque and *fin-de-siécle* buildings seldom higher than six storeys so if you're looking for a meal with scenery, consider a water feature. The choices range from river to lake and even pond. In Pest, both **Spoon** (p50) and **Vogue** (p54) are on boats moored in the Danube; the latter offers views of the river seldom seen. The lakeside tables at **Robinson** (below) in City Park are coveted, but if you're willing to downsize head for **Malomtó** (p48) overlooking a tiny lake (pond really) in, appropriately enough, Víziváros (Watertown).

Robinson makes the most of its leafy park surrounds

Entertainment

Budapest has a huge choice of things to do and places to go after dark – from opera and folk dancing to jazz and meat-market clubs. It's almost never difficult getting tickets or getting in; the hard part is deciding what to do.

The best sources of information are the weekly freebie **PestiEst** (www.est.hu in Hungarian), published every Thursday and available from bars, cinemas and fast-food joints, and the more thorough weekly – with everything from clubs and films to exhibitions and classical music – **Pesti Műsor** (www.pestimusor.hu in Hungarian), available from newsstands every Thursday for 149Ft. The English-language weekly *Budapest Sun* also lists events and concerts in its useful Style supplement. A welcome arrival is *Mr Gordonsky's Budapest City Spy Map*, a hip little publication with all sorts of insider's tips. It's available free at pubs and bars.

The best website for happenings in Budapest is **BTO** (www.budapestinfo.hu). **Pestiside** (www.pestiside.hu), subtitled 'The Daily Dish of Cosmopolitan Budapest', is an acerbic and often very funny take on the capital, and includes lots of listings and reviews of what's on.

There are no concentrated nightlife areas on the Buda side, unless you count sedate (some might say comatose) Castle Hill or the rather dispersed II Moszkva tér (4, A3). The Pest side, on the other hand, has all sorts of strips – from the ultratouristed V Duna korzó (6, A4), along the river, with pricey (and very ordinary) eateries and watering holes, to leafy VI Andrássy út (6, B3) – always a sophisticated choice for a night out. But the two main areas are übertrendy VI Liszt Ferenc tér (6, C3), where you'll have to duel to the death for a spot under the plane trees, and IX Ráday utca (6, B6), a rather subdued semi-pedestrianised street in Józsefváros full of pubs and bars.

Theatres line the streets of Nagymező utca, also known as Budapest's 'Broadway'

SPECIAL EVENTS

January
New Year's Day Concert (www.hungariakoncert.hu) Annual event usually held in Pesti Vigadó on 1 January to welcome in the new year

International Circus Festival (www.maciva. hu) Biennial (2008, 2010 etc) event held under the big top of the Municipal Great Circus (5, D1) in late January

February
Opera Ball (www.operabal.com) Prestigious annual event at the Hungarian State Opera House

March
Budapest Spring Festival (www.festivalcity.hu) The capital's largest and most important cultural festival

April
National Dance House Meeting & Fair (www.tanchaz.hu) Hungary's biggest *táncház* (p65) held over two days at the Budapest Sportaréna

May
Budapest Early Music Forum (www.festivalcity.hu) Classical music as it was played when first composed

June
Danube Folklore Carnival (www.dunaart.hu) Pan-Hungarian international carnival of folk dance and music, world music and modern dance, held over 10 days

Bridge Festival (www.festivalcity.hu) Day-long festival of music, dance and street theatre

Ferencváros Summer Festival (www.festivalcity.hu) Music and dance performed by local groups in the streets of district IX

Budapest Fair (www.festivalcity.hu) Citywide performances marking the departure of Soviet troops from Hungary in 1991

Museum Night (www.museum.hu/events) Two dozen museums across town with their doors open from 6pm until the wee hours

August
Formula One Hungarian Grand Prix (www.hungaroring.hu) Hungary's premier sporting event, held in Mogyoród, 24km northeast of the capital

Sziget Music Festival (www.sziget.hu) One of the biggest and most popular music festivals in Europe, held on Hajógyár Island

Crafts Celebration (www.nesz.hu) Craft stalls and workshops on Castle Hill, run by prominent Hungarian artists

Jewish Summer Festival (www.jewishfestival.hu) Jewish culture showcased through exhibitions, gastronomy and a book and film week

September
Budapest International Wine Fair (www.winefestival.hu) Wines exhibited on Castle Hill by Hungary's foremost winemakers

October
Budapest International Marathon (www.budapestmarathon.com) Eastern Europe's most celebrated foot race

Budapest Autumn Festival (www.festivalcity.hu) Cultural events at venues throughout the city until early November

December
New Year's Gala & Ball (www.viparts.hu) Gala dinner and ball held at the Hungarian State Opera House on 31 December

BARS

Buda

Erzsébet Híd Eszpresszó (5, A5)
The 'Elizabeth Bridge Espresso Bar' is a wonderful old dive with a large terrace and views of the bridge. Most people call it Platán in honour of the big plane tree sheltering the outdoor tables.
☎ 214 2785 ✉ I Döbrentei tér 1 ⏲ 10am-10pm 🚊 19

Kisrabló (5, B6)
This pub is close to the university (and to many of Budapest's hostels), and is thus very popular with students; it's an attractive and well-run place.
☎ 209 1588 ✉ XI Zenta utca 3 ⏲ 11-2am Mon-Sat, noon-2am Sun 🚊 18, 19, 47, 49

Lánchíd Söröző (4, C4)
The 'Chain Bridge Pub', at the southern end of Fő utca, has a wonderful retro Magyar feel, with old movie posters and advertisements on the walls, and red-checked cloths on the tables. Friendly service too.
☎ 214 3144 ✉ I Fő utca 4 ⏲ 10am-midnight 🚌 86

Oscar American Bar (4, A3)
The décor is cinema-inspired – film memorabilia on the wood-panelled walls, leather directors' chairs – and the beautiful crowd often act like they're on camera. The potent cocktails (some 150 of them) go down a treat. There's music most nights.
☎ 212 8017 ✉ I Ostrom utca 14 ⏲ 5pm-2am Mon-Thu, 5pm-4am Fri & Sat year-round, 5pm-2am Sun Nov-May only Ⓜ M2 Moszkva tér

Poco Loco (4, off B1)
At the corner of Harcsa utca and Frankel Leó út on the way to Óbuda, this one-time seamy place has cleaned up its act; however, it remains interesting. There's live music some nights.
☎ 326 1357 ✉ II Harcsa utca 1 ⏲ 11am-midnight 🚊 17

Pest

Cha Cha Cha (6, B5)
In the underpass at Kálvin tér metro station, this is a campy, groovy café bar with distressed-looking furniture, a very unusual crowd and bopping from the end of the week. It's a great place to meet people, and it gets busier here in the wee hours than the entire station does during the day.
☎ 215 0545 ⏲ 8-3am Mon-Thu, 10-4am Fri & Sat Sep-May, 9am-11pm Jun-Aug Ⓜ M3 Kálvin tér

Champs Sport Bar (6, C4)
Owned by five Olympic medallists, Champs is the place for sports fans and the vicarious, with two huge screens and 35 TVs. There's a wide choice of low-fat 'fitness meals' along with the less healthy favourites of armchair athletes.
☎ 413 1655 ✉ VII Dohány utca 20 ☎ noon-midnight Sun-Thu, noon-2am Fri & Sat Ⓜ M2 Astoria

The friendly Lánchíd Söröző

Darshan Udvar (6, C5)
This cavernous complex of two bars, a restaurant and a courtyard-terrace vegetarian café is a great escape from the bars of VI Liszt Ferenc tér and IX Ráday utca. In fact, Krúdy utca may be poised to take over as Budapest's next after-hours strip.
☎ 266 5541 ✉ VIII Krúdy utca 7 ⏲ 11-1am Mon-Fri, 6pm-1am Sat & Sun 🚊 4, 6

EGÉSZSÉGÉRE!

Drinking is an important part of social life in the capital of a country that has produced wine and fruit brandies for thousands of years. Consumption is high; only the Luxembourgeois and Irish drink more alcohol per capita in Europe than the Hungarians. (It means 'to your health', by the way.)

THE HEAT IS ON

During Budapest's (usually) long and hot summer, *kertek* (literally 'gardens') empty out even the most popular indoor bars and clubs. Venues and locations change from year to year; check Pestiside (www.pestiside.hu) for the most recent.

Café del Rio (5, B6; ☎ 06 30 297 2158; XI Goldmann György tér 1; ☻ 2pm-4.30am; ⛟ 4, 6) Stylish but not up itself, with a pseudo tropical/carnival theme

Cha Cha Cha Terasz (3, A5; ☎ 215 0545; XIII Margitsziget; ☻ 4pm-4am; 🚌 26 or ⛟ 4, 6) An attitude-free venue with great music and dance space

Holdudvar (6, C5; ☎ 485 5270; VIII Múzeum körút 6-8; ☻ 8-4am; Ⓜ M2 Astoria) On the grounds of the city's largest university, with a split personality: earnest and coffee-drinking, wild and out of control

Mokka Cuka (4, off B1; ☎ 453 2120; www.mokkacuka.hu; III Óbuda Hajógyári-sziget; ☻ 2pm-4am; 🚃 HÉV Filatorigát) On the island that attracts the capital's beautiful people, showcasing great indie DJs

Szimpla Kert (6, C4; ☎ 321 5880, 06 20 248 1968; www.szimpla.hu; VII Kazinczy 14; ☻ noon-midnight; trolleybus 74) A simple, low-key affair that keeps itself to itself

Szóda Udvar (6, A4; ☎ 461 0007; V József nádor tér 1; ☻ 2pm-4am; Ⓜ M1/2/3 Deák Ferenc tér) A well-heeled venue pulling in a rather subdued crowd that lets loose on the dance floor

Zöld Pardon (5, B6; XI Goldmann György tér; ☻ 9-6am; ⛟ 4, 6) A rocker's paradise opposite the Café del Rio

Janis Pub (6, B5)
Close to the university, this ever-popular pub is a shrine to the late, great Janis 'Pearl' Joplin and usually a stop for a quick one or two on the way to somewhere else. But some linger here for the choice of five imported beers on draught and the darts.
☎ 266 2619 ✉ V Királyi Pál utca 8 ☻ 4pm-2am Mon-Thu, 4pm-3am Fri & Sat Ⓜ M3 Kálvin tér

Kultiplex (6, C6)
This huge complex has something for everyone – performance space, cinema, grill restaurant, great DJs, theme parties – and a simple inside/outside bar, where you can enjoy an unreconstructed drink.
☎ 219 0706 ✉ IX Kinizsi utca 28 ☻ 10-5am Ⓜ M3 Ferenc körút

Picasso Point (6, B2)
A stalwart of the Budapest entertainment scene, this is a laid-back place for a drink and good for meeting people. Great décor.
☎ 312 1727 ✉ VI Hajós utca 31 ☻ noon-midnight Mon-Wed, noon-2am Thu & Fri, 4pm-2am Sat Ⓜ M3 Arany János utca

Pótkulcs (6, B2)
The 'Spare Key' is a wonderful little drinking venue, with a varied menu of live music from 9.30pm most nights and *táncház* (see p65) at 8pm every Tuesday. The small central courtyard is a wonderful place to chill out in summer.
☎ 269 1050 ✉ VI Csengery utca 65/b ☻ 5pm-1.30am

Cha Cha Cha Terasz on Margaret Island is just as cool as its underground sister bar, shown here

Sun-Wed, 5pm-2.30am Thu-Sat (M) M3 Nyugati pályaudvar

Szimpla (6, C3)

This is a distressed-looking, very unflashy three-floor venue, and it's just a hop, skip and a tumble from the stilettos south of Liszt Ferenc tér. There's live music three nights a week.

☎ 321 9119, 321 5880 ✉ VII Kertész utca 48 ⏲ 10-2am Sep-May, noon-midnight Jun-Oct 🚃 4, 6

TRADITIONAL CAFÉS

Buda

Angelika (4, C3)

Angelika is a charming café attached to an 18th-century church, with a lovely terrace overlooking the Danube. The food is just so-so; come here for the cakes and the views.

☎ 212 3784 ✉ I Batthyány tér 7 ⏲ 9-2am (M) M2 Batthyány tér

Auguszt (4, A3)

Tucked away on the 1st floor of a building behind the Fény utca market and Mammut shopping mall, this is the original Auguszt café (there are imitators), and sells only its own shop-made cakes, pastries and biscuits.

☎ 356 8931, 316 3817 ✉ II Fény utca 8, 1st fl ⏲ 10am-6pm Tue-Fri, 9am-6pm Sat (M) M2 Moszkva tér

Ruszwurm (4, B4)

This is the perfect place for coffee and cakes on Castle

CAFÉ SOCIETY

Old-style cafés, some of which date back as much as a century and a half, abound in Budapest. The Turks introduced coffee to Hungary in the early 16th century, and the coffee house was an essential part of the social scene here long before it was in Vienna or Paris. In the final decades of the Austro-Hungarian empire, Budapest had some 600 cafés. A new breed of café – all polished chrome, halogen lighting and straight lines – now coexists with the more traditional cafés.

Hill, though it can get pretty crowded and be difficult to get a seat.

☎ 375 5284 ✉ I Szentháromság utca 7 ⏲ 9am-8pm 🚌 16 or Várbusz

Pest

Centrál Kávéház (6, B5)

This grande dame, which reopened a few years ago after extensive renovations, is still jostling to reclaim her title as the place to sit and look intellectual in Pest.

☎ 266 4572, 266 2110 ✉ V Károlyi Mihály utca ⏲ 8am-midnight (M) M3 Ferenciek tere

Gerbeaud (6, A4)

This is the most famous of the famous cafés in Budapest – bar none. Founded in 1858, it has been a fashionable meeting place for the city's elite on the northern side of Pest's busiest square since 1870. A visit is mandatory.

☎ 429 9020 ✉ V Vörösmarty tér 7-8 ⏲ 9am-9pm (M) M1 Vörösmarty tér

Lukács (6, C2)

This café is dressed up in the finest of divine decadence – all mirrors and gold and soft piano music (on weekday evenings) with a nonsmoking section too. The

Sip your coffee in the decadent surrounds of Lukács café

selection of cakes is small but good; try the creamy *Lukács szelet* (Lukács slice).

☎ 302 8747 ✉ VI Andrássy út 70 🕑 9am-8pm Mon-Fri, 10am-8pm Sat & Sun Ⓜ M1 Vörösmarty utca

Művész (6, B3)
Almost opposite the State Opera House, the 'Artist', here since 1898, is a more interesting place to people-watch than most cafés (especially from the terrace), though its cakes are not what they used to be, with the exception of the *almás torta* (apple cake).

☎ 352 1337 ✉ VI Andrássy út 29 🕑 9am-11.45pm Ⓜ M1 Opera

MODERN CAFÉS

Buda
Café Miró (4, B4)
A personal favourite on Castle Hill, Miró has Med-coloured walls and furniture, snacks and cakes, and local artwork

and photography on the walls. It's open on two sides.

☎ 201 5573 ✉ I Úri utca 30 🕑 9am-midnight 🚌 16 or Várbusz

Café Ponyvaragény (5, A6)
'Pulp Fiction' is a great place

Get comfortable at the Café Ponyvaragény

that's supposed to be a local secret but – alas – is no longer. The old books and fringed lampshades are a nice touch, and the coffee is some of the best in town.

☎ 209 5255 ✉ XI Bercsényi utca 5 🕑 10am-midnight Mon-Sat, 2pm-midnight Sun 🚊 18, 19, 47, 49

Pest
Café Vian (6, C3)
This comfortable café – done up in warm peach tones and serving breakfast all day – remains the anchor tenant on the sunny side of 'the tér', courted by Pest's arty aristocracy.

☎ 268 1154 ✉ VI Liszt Ferenc tér 9 🕑 9-1am Ⓜ M1 Oktogon

Gerlóczy Kávéház (6, B4)
This wonderful retro-style café looks out onto one of Pest's most attractive little

squares, and serves excellent snacks and light meals, including a cheese plate sent over from the Nagy Tamás cheese shop (p53) around the corner.
☎ 235 0953 ✉ V Gerlóczy utca 1 ◷ 7am-11pm Mon-Fri, 8am-11pm Sat & Sun 🚊 47, 49

Két Szerecsen (6, B3)
Not on the square but close enough, the very relaxed 'Two Moors' serves both main meals and decent breakfasts, as well as coffee.
☎ 343 1984 ✉ VI Nagymező utca 14 ◷ 8-1am Sun-Thu, 9-1am Fri & Sat

Negro (6, A3)
This stylish café just behind the basilica (views!) attracts Budapest's über-trendy crowd, dressed to the nines and sipping the latest concoction.
☎ 302 0136 ✉ V Szent István tér 11 ◷ 8am-midnight Sun, 8-1am Mon-Wed, 8-3am Thu & Fri, 8-4am Sat Ⓜ M3 Arany János utca

CLUBS

Bank Dance Hall (6, B1)
In the southern wing of Nyugati train station next to McDonald's, this enormous disco has rhythm and blues on the 1st floor, house and trance on the 2nd, dance on the 3rd and funk-house (a Hungarian thing) on the 4th. Lots of young suburban types reeking of cologne and on the prowl.
☎ 06 20 344 4888 ✉ VI Teréz körút 55 ◷ 10pm-4am Sun-Thu,

Strut your stuff at the popular Club Vittula

10pm-5am Fri & Sat Ⓜ M3 Nyugati pályaudvar

Club Vittula (6, C4)
Probably the best place to get drunk and dance in Budapest at the moment, with cutting-edge DJs and cheap Slovakian blond (beer that is). Need we say more?
☎ 06 20 527 7069 ✉ VII Kertész utca 4 ◷ 6pm-dawn Sep-Jun Ⓜ M2 Blaha Lujza tér 🚊 4, 6

Kaméleon (4, A3)
This throbbing club in the newer wing of Buda's massive Mammut shopping mall is a true 'chameleon', with a different party in swing every night of the week – from La Noche Cubana on Friday to live bands on Monday.
☎ 345 8547 ✉ Mammut II, 4th fl, II Lövőház utca 2-6 ◷ 5pm-midnight Sun-Thu,

5pm-3am Fri & Sat Ⓜ M3 Moszkva tér

Piaf (6, B2)
Piaf is the place to go when everything else slows down. There's dancing and action well into the new day. Most of the action – and characters – are in the smoky cavern below.
☎ 312 3823 ✉ VI Nagymező utca 25 ◷ 7pm-6am Ⓜ M3 Arany János utca 🚊 trolleybus 70, 78

Sark Café (6, C3)
This popular alternative music pub and club on three floors has a big cellar with a dance floor where bands occasionally perform.
☎ 06 30 282 9625 ✉ VII Klauzál tér 14 ◷ 10-3am Sun-Thu, 10-5am Fri & Sat 🚊 4, 6

Süss Fel Nap (6, A1)
Attracting a student crowd, this cellar club hosts lots of student bands and visiting talent. It's a lot of fun and less expensive than many of the other clubs. It's one of the few places in town offering a two-for-one happy hour (5pm to 8pm).
☎ 374 3329 ⌧ V Honvéd utca 40 🕑 5pm-5am
🚋 4, 6

GAY & LESBIAN VENUES

Action Bar (6, B5)
The name says it all. Take the usual precautions and have a ball. Strippers and dancers make appearances every night from about midnight.
☎ 266 9148 ⌧ V Magyar utca 42 🕑 9pm-4am
Ⓜ M3 Kálvin tér

Angel (6, C4)
Angel, also known by its Hungarian name, Angyal, is Budapest's flagship gay club, even since its big move in 2005 after something like a decade. It welcomes girls on Friday and Sunday, but boys only on Saturday.
☎ 351 6490 ⌧ VII Kazinczy utca 2 🕑 10pm-5am Fri-Sun Ⓜ M2 Astoria

Café Eklektika (6, B4)
While there are no specifically lesbian bars in Budapest, Café Eklektika comes the closest, and attracts a very mixed crowd. Lots of canned jazz and the like.
☎ 266 1226 ⌧ V Semmelweis utca 21 🕑 noon-midnight Mon-Fri,

5pm-midnight Sat & Sun
🚋 47, 49

Club Bohemian Alibi (6, D6)
This club attracts ladies and gentlemen, and anything in between. It's the preferred watering hole of Budapest's burgeoning TV population, so if you're into cross-dressing or cross-dressers, this is the place to be.
☎ 06 20 314 1959 ⌧ IX Üllői út 45-47 🕑 4pm-4am Sun-Thu, 9pm-4am Fri & Sat Ⓜ M3 Ferenc körút

Upside Down (6, B3)
Below a coffee shop of the same name on the southern side of Podmaniczky tér, this is one of the hottest new gay clubs in town.
☎ 06 20 982 2884 ⌧ V Podmaniczky Frigyes tér 1 🕑 8pm-4am or 5am Ⓜ M3 Arany János utca

CLASSICAL MUSIC

The **Koncert Kalendárium** (www.koncert kalendarium.hu) highlights all concerts in Budapest monthly, and most nights you'll have several to choose from.

Budapest Congress Centre (4, A6)
This modern conference centre in Buda moonlights as a concert hall, and has recently undergone a major renovation – supposedly to improve its poor acoustics. Big-ticket galas and opening nights are frequently held here.
☎ information 372 5700, tickets 372 5429 🖳 www.

bcc.hu ⌧ XII Jagelló út 1-3
🚌 8, 112

Duna Palota (6, A3)
This elaborate 'palace' diagonally opposite the main Central European University building hosts light classical music and touristy musical revues in summer. Its biggest drawcard is its folk-dance performances.
☎ 235 5500, 317 2790 ⌧ V Zrínyi utca 5 🚌 15

Ferenc Liszt Academy of Music (6, C3)
A block southeast of Oktogon, what's usually just called the 'music academy' was built in 1907. It attracts students from all over the world, and is one of the top venues for concerts. The interior, with large and small concert halls richly embellished with Zsolnay porcelain and frescoes, is worth a look even if you're not attending a performance.
☎ 342 0179 🖳 www.zeneakade mia.hu ⌧ VI Liszt Ferenc tér 8 🕑 ticket office 10am-8pm Mon-Fri, 2-8pm Sat & Sun Ⓜ M1 Oktogon

Palace of Arts (5, off C6)
The main concert halls in this palatial arts centre by the Danube, just opposite the National Theatre, are the 1700-seat National Concert Hall and the smaller Festival Theatre, accommodating up to 450 people. Both are purported to have the best acoustics in Budapest.
☎ information 555 3000, tickets 555 3301 🖳 www.mupa.hu ⌧ IX Komor Marcell utca 1 🕑 ticket office 1-6pm Mon-Sat, 10am-3pm Sun 🚋 2, 2A

Pesti Vigadó (6, A4)
This Romantic-style hall, built in 1865 and facing the Danube to the west of Vörösmarty tér, is a popular venue for concerts, dance performances and other cultural events. It was badly damaged during WWII and, though the original style of the exterior was retained, the interior is all new and has been recently renovated.
☎ 318 9903, 318 9167
✉ V Vigadó tér 2
Ⓜ M1 Vörösmarty tér
🚋 2, 2A

FOLK & TRADITIONAL MUSIC

Almássy tér Recreation Centre (6, D3)
This venue west of Keleti train station has just about anything that's in and/or interesting, from rock and blues to jazz, but especially folk music. There's a Hungarian dance house every second Saturday at 7.30pm.
☎ 352 1572 ✉ VII Almássy tér 6 🚋 trolleybus 74

Aranytíz Cultural Centre (6, A3)
With programmes from 5pm on Saturday, frequently running to well after 2am, this gleaming new cultural centre in the Northern Inner Town hosts the incomparable Kalamajka Táncház, one of Budapest's most popular *táncház* nights (see above).
☎ 354 3400, 311 2248 ✉ V Arany János utca 10 🚋 15

Fonó Buda Music House (5, off A6)
Fonó Buda has regular

HUNGARIAN FOLK & KLEZMER MUSIC

Violins, zithers, hurdy-gurdies, bagpipes and lutes are the instruments of Hungarian folk. Watch out for Muzsikás (with the inimitable Márta Sebestyén, or on her own); Ghymes, a Hungarian folk band from Slovakia; Vujicsics, with elements of South Slav music in the mix; and the energetic fiddler Félix Lajkoa from the Magyar-speaking area of northern Serbia.

Attending a *táncház* (literally 'dance house') is an excellent way to hear Hungarian folk music, and even to learn to dance. Consult one of the publications mentioned on p57, or check out the website of the Dance House Guild (www.tanchaz.hu), for times and locations.

Klezmer – traditional Yiddish music of similar origin to Gypsy and Roma music – is currently going through something of a renaissance in Budapest. Once closely associated with Central European folk music, *klezmer* dance bands were led by the violin and cymbalom until WWI; the influence of Yiddish theatre and the first wax recordings inspired a switch to the clarinet. The best local *klezmorim* belong to the Budapest Klezmer Band; see www.budapestklezmer.hu for dates and venues.

The Folklór Centrum in the **Municipal Cultural House** (Fővárosi Művelődési Háza; 5, off A6; ☎ 203 3868; XI Fehérvári út 47; 🚋 41, 47) presents folk music every Friday at 7.30pm, and the **Marczibányi tér Cultural Centre** (Marczibányi téri Művelődési Központ; 4, A2; ☎ 212 0803, 212 2820; II Marczibányi tér 5/a; 🚋 4, 6, 49) has Hungarian, Moldavian and Slovakian dance and music every Wednesday starting from 8pm.

programmes at 8pm on Wednesday and the second Friday of each month, as well as concerts by big-name bands throughout each month; it's one of the best venues in town for this sort of thing. Consult the website for more details.
☎ 206 5300 🖥 www.fono.hu ✉ XI Sztregova utca 3 🚋 41, 47

JAZZ & BLUES

Columbus Jazzklub
(5, A4)
On a boat moored in the Danube just north of V Vigadó tér, opposite the Budapest Inter-Continental Hotel, this club has transformed itself from being 'just another Irish pub' to a jazz club of note, with big-name local and international bands.
☎ 266 9013 🖳 www. majazz.hu ✉ V Pesti alsó rakpart 🕑 noon-midnight 🚋 2, 2A

Cotton Club (6, B2)
This centrally located restaurant and nightclub with gangster-and-moll décor (complete with cigar room) has live jazz – or let's say 'jazz lite' – nightly at 7.30pm or 8pm.
☎ 354 0886 🖳 www. cottonclub.hu ✉ VI Jókai utca 26 🕑 noon-midnight Mon-Sat 🚋 4, 6

Fat Mo's Music Club
(6, B5)
With a speakeasy Prohibition theme, and enough beer and booze to fill Bonnie and Clyde (with bullets, that is), FM's has live jazz (and sometimes country) from 9pm or 9.30pm daily. DJs take over at midnight from Thursday to Saturday.
☎ 267 3199 ✉ V Nyáry Pál utca 11 🕑 noon-2am Mon & Tue, noon-3am Wed, noon-4am Thu & Fri, 6pm-4am Sat, 6pm-2am Sun Ⓜ M3 Ferenciek tere 🚌 15

Jazz Garden (6, B6)
This is a sophisticated venue with traditional, vocal and Latin jazz, and odd décor – a faux cellar 'garden' with street lamps and a night 'sky' bedecked with blinking stars. Book a table in the dining room; music starts here at 9.30pm.
☎ 266 7364 ✉ V Veres Pálné utca 44/a 🕑 6pm-1am Sun-Thu, 6pm-2am Fri & Sat 🚋 47, 49

ROCK & POP

A38 Hajó (5, C6)
Moored on the Buda side just south of Petőfi Bridge, the 'A38 Ship' is a decommissioned Ukrainian stone hauler from 1968 that has been reinvented as a party venue. It's so cool, it's hot in summer; and the hold, well, rocks throughout the year.
☎ 464 3940 🖳 www.a38. hu ✉ XI Műegyetem rakpart 🕑 11am-midnight, later on event nights 🚋 4 or 6

Gödör Klub (6, A4)
This venue in the old bus bays below Erzsébet tér in central Pest is a real mixed bag, offering everything from folk and jazz, but especially rock.
☎ 06 20 943 5464 ✉ Erzsébet tér 🕑 9am-late Ⓜ 1/2/3 Deák Ferenc tér

Jailhouse (6, D6)
This tiny venue with a friendly atmosphere has underground DJs and live music. It's an excellent place to part ways from the usual choice of venues. It hosts a lesbian night on the first Friday of the month.
☎ 218 1368, 06 30 989 4905 ✉ IX Tűzoltó utca

Fat Mo's is a music venue, bar and restaurant rolled into one

22 ⊗ 10pm-5am Fri & Sat
Ⓜ M3 Ferenc körút

Wigwam Rock & Blues Club (5, off A6)
This place with the wacky name is one of the best of its kind in Hungary, and hosts some big-name Hungarian rock and blues bands on Friday and Saturday nights.
☎ 208 5569 ⊠ XI Fehérvári utca 202 ⊗ 8pm-5am ⓐ 41, 47

THEATRE, OPERA & DANCE

The interior of the Hungarian State Opera House

Budapest Operetta (6, B3)
The operettas, with their OTT staging and costumes, are always a riot, especially campy ones like the *Queen of the Csárdás* by Imre Kálmán.
☎ 472 2030, 312 4866 ⌨ www.operettszinhaz.hu ⊠ VI Nagymező utca 17 ⊗ ticket office 10am-7pm Mon-Fri, 1-7pm Sat & Sun Ⓜ M1 Opera

Comedy Theatre (6, A1)
The attractive little theatre, roughly in the middle of the Szent István körút section of the 'Big Ring Road', is the venue for comedies and musicals.
☎ information 329 2340, tickets 329 3920 ⊠ XIII Szent István körút 14 ⊗ ticket office 10am-6pm Mon-Thu, 10am-5pm Fri ⓐ 4, 6

Hungarian State Opera House (6, B3)
The gorgeous neo-Renaissance opera house should be visited at least once – to admire the incredibly rich decoration inside as much as to view a performance and hear the perfect acoustics. Visits are guided (see p25).
☎ information 353 0170, tickets 332 7914 ⌨ www.opera.hu ⊠ VI Andrássy út 22 ⊗ ticket office 11am-7pm Mon-Sat, 11am-1pm & 4-7pm Sun Ⓜ M1 Opera

József Katona Theatre (6, B5)
The best-known theatre in Hungary, this place is supported mainly by the city of Budapest. Its studio theatre, Kamara, has among the best troupes in the country.
☎ 318 3725 ⌨ www.szinhaz.hu/katona ⊠ V Petőfi Sándor utca 6 ⊗ ticket office 10am-7pm Mon-Fri, 2-7pm Sat & Sun Ⓜ M3 Ferenciek tere

JUST THE TICKET
The most important and/or useful booking agencies in Budapest include those listed below. You can book almost everything online through www.jegymester.hu or www.kulturinfo.hu.
Central Ticket Office (Központi Jegyiroda; 6, B3; ☎ 267 9737, 267 1267; VI Andrássy út 15) The busiest theatrical agency
Symphony Ticket Office (Szimfonikus Jegyiroda; 6, B3; ☎ 302 3841; VI Nagymező utca 19) Philharmonic and other classical-music concerts
Ticket Express (6, B3; ☎ information 312 0000, reservations 06 30 303 0999; www.tex.hu; VI Andrássy út 18) The largest ticket-office network with eight outlets, including a Józsefváros branch (6, D5; ☎ 334 0369; MCD Zeneáruház, VIII József körút 50)

Merlin Theatre (6, B4)
This theatre in the heart of Pest stages numerous plays in English, often performed by the theatre's own Atlantis Company or the local Madhouse troupe. It's usually pretty serious stuff, with little scenery and few props.
☎ 318 9338, 266 4632
🖳 www.merlinszinhaz. hu ✉ V Gerlóczy utca 4
Ⓜ M1/2/3 Deák Ferenc tér
🚊 47, 49

National Dance Theatre (4, C5)
The National Dance Theatre on Castle Hill hosts at some point every troupe in the city, including the two ballet companies and the Honvéd Ensemble – one of the city's best folk troupes and now experimenting with modern choreography as well.
☎ information 201 4407, tickets 375 8649 🖳 www. nemzetitancszinhaz.hu
✉ I Színház utca 1-3
🕐 ticket office 1-6pm
🚌 16 or Várbusz

Trafó House of Contemporary Arts (6, D6)
This is the best stage on

The Uránia National Cinema (opposite) attracts coffee friends as well as film fans

which to see modern dance, including a good pull of international acts.
☎ information 456 2045, tickets 215 1600 🖳 www. trafo.hu ✉ IX Liliom utca 41
Ⓜ M3 Ferenc körút

CINEMAS

For listings, see the *Budapest Sun* newspaper, *PestiEst* or *Pesti Műsor* (p57).

Corvin Film Palace (6, D6)
This place saw a lot of action during the 1956 revolution, and led a different sort of revolution four decades later – the introduction of state-of-the-art sound

systems and comfortable seating. It has now been fantastically renovated, and is worth a visit. Note the two wonderful reliefs outside and the monument to the *Pesti srácok*, the heroic 'kids from Pest' who fought and died here in 1956.
☎ 459 5050 ✉ VIII Corvin köz 1 Ⓜ M3 Ferenc körút

Művész (6, B2)
The 'Artist' shows, appropriately enough, arty and cult films, but not exclusively so.
☎ 332 6726 ✉ VI Teréz körút 30 Ⓜ M1 Oktogon
🚊 4, 6

Örökmozgó Film Museum (6, C3)
Part of the Hungarian Film Institute, this cinema (whose mouthful of a name vaguely translates as 'moving picture') shows an excellent assortment of foreign classic films in their original languages.
☎ 342 2167 ✉ VII Erzsébet körút 39 🚊 4, 6

Szindbád (6, A1)
This place, named after the seminal 1971 film by director

FILMED IN BUDAPEST

- *Kontroll* (*Inspection*; Hungary, 2003) Hungarian-American director Nimród Antal
- *Evita* (USA, 1996)
- *Ein Lied von Liebe und Tod* (*Gloomy Sunday*; Germany/Hungary, 1999) German director Rolf Schübel
- *Amerikai Rapszódia* (*American Rhapsody*; Hungary, 2001) by Éva Gardos
- *Napoléon* (France, 2002) by Yves Simoneau

Zoltán Huszárik, shows good Hungarian and foreign films with subtitles.

☎ 349 2773 ✉ XIII Szent István körút 16 🚊 4, 6

Uránia National Cinema
(6, C4)
This Art Deco/neo-Moorish extravaganza is another tarted-up film palace. It has an excellent café on the 1st floor, which is an attraction in itself.

☎ 486 3413 ✉ VIII Rákóczi út 21 🚊 7, 7A

SPORT

Football

There are four premier-league football teams in Budapest. Kispest Honvéd plays at the city's **József Bozsik Stadium** (☎ 282 9791, 282 9789); MTK at **Hungária Stadium** (☎ 219 0300), and UTE at **UTE Stadium** (☎ 369 7333). But no club dominates Hungarian football like Ferencváros (FTC), the country's most loved and hated team. You can watch them play at the **FTC Stadium** (☎ 215 1013; IX Könyves Kálmán körút 26; Ⓜ M3 Népliget), near Népliget (People's Park). The daily *Nemzeti Sport* (*National Sport*; 99Ft) has the match schedules.

Horse Racing

Kincsem Park (☎ 433 0522; www.kincsempark. com; X Albertirsai út 2; Ⓜ M2 Pillangó utca) is the place to go for both *ügető* (trotting) and *galopp* (flat racing). Schedules can change, but in general three trotting meetings of 10 to 11 races take place each week, usually at 3pm on Saturday and Sunday, and at 4pm or 5pm on Wednesday all year round. Flat racing usually takes place from 2pm on Thursday and Sunday between May and early November.

Motor Racing

Reintroduced in 1986 following a hiatus of half a century, the **Formula 1 Hungarian Grand Prix** (☎ 28-444 444; www. hungaroring.hu) takes place in August at the Hungaroring at Mogyoród, 24km northeast of Budapest. The only seats with views of the starting grid are Super Gold ones, and cost €400 for the weekend; cheaper are Gold (€300 to €320), which are near the pit lane, and Silver (€225 to €250) tickets. Standing room costs €110 for the weekend, €100 for Sunday.

Water Polo

The **Hungarian Water Polo Association** (MVLSZ; ☎ 412 0041) is based at the Alfréd Hajós National Sports Pool (p85) on Margaret Island. Matches take place here and at two other pools – the Béla Komjádi in Buda and the BVSC in Pest from September to May. If you want to see a match or watch the lads in training in summer, call the MVLSZ for times and dates, or get someone to check schedules for you in the *Nemzeti Sport* newspaper.

The Ferencváros team playing a match at the FTC Stadium

Sleeping

Accommodation in Budapest runs the gamut from hostels in converted flats and private rooms in far-flung housing estates to luxury *pensions* and five-star properties charging upwards of €300 a night. **Hotels** (*szállók* or *szállodák*) can be anything from the rapidly disappearing run-down old socialist-era hovels to luxurious five-star palaces.

Hungary's **private rooms** (*fizetővendég szolgálat*; 'paying-guest service') can be great deals and relatively cheap (6500Ft to 8000Ft a double), although you may have to try several offices to get a room in the centre of town. Individuals on the streets outside the main train stations may offer you a private room, but their prices are usually higher than those asked by the agencies, and there is no quality control. Among the best agencies are **Ibusz** (5, B4; ☎ 485 2700; www.ibusz.hu; V Ferenciek tere 10; ☺ 9am-6pm Mon-Fri, 9am-1pm Sat; Ⓜ M3 Ferenciek tere), **Vista** (5, B3; ☎ 429 9751; www.vista.hu; VI Paulay Ede utca 2; ☺ 9am-6.30pm Mon-Fri, 9am-2.30pm Sat; Ⓜ M1/2/3 Deák Ferenc tér) and **U Tours** (5, E3; ☎ 303 9818; Platform 6, Keleti train station; ☺ 7am-8pm).

Accommodation at Budapest's **hostels** (*ifjúsági szállók*) is available all year round, but during the university summer holidays (generally mid-June or July to late August), private outfits rent vacant rooms from the universities and turn them into hostels. Competition is fierce, and there are several hostel operators (see p73), so you can afford to shop around a bit.

The low season runs roughly from mid-October or November to March (not including the Christmas and New Year holidays). The high season is the rest of the year – a lengthy seven months or so – when prices can increase by as much as 30%. Almost without exception, the rate quoted for hostels and hotels includes breakfast. Some top-end hotels in Budapest do not include the 15% VAT in their listed room rates.

ROOM RATES

The categories indicate the cost per night of a standard double room in high season. (Note that many hotels quote their rates in euros.)

Deluxe	over 50,500Ft (€200)
Top End	25,500Ft (€104) to 50,000Ft (€198)
Midrange	12,500Ft (€50) to 25,000Ft (€102)
Budget	under 12,000Ft (€49)

The Four Seasons Gresham Palace Hotel, restored to its Art Nouveau splendour

DELUXE

Art'otel Budapest (4, C4)
Buda – Víziváros

This minimalist hotel wouldn't look out of place in London or New York. What makes this 165-room place unique is that it cobbles together a seven-storey modern building (views of the castle and the Danube) and an 18th-century baroque building; they're separated by a leafy courtyard-cum-atrium.

☎ 487 9487 🖳 www.artotel.hu ✉ I Bem rakpart 16-19 🚊 19 🚌 86

Four Seasons Gresham Palace Hotel (5, A3)
Pest – Inner Town

This magnificent 179-room hotel has been created out of the long-empty Art Nouveau Gresham Palace (1907). No expense was spared to piece back together the palace's Zsolnay tiles, famous wrought-iron Peacock Gates and splendid mosaics; the hotel is truly worthy of its name.

☎ 268 6000 🖳 www.fourseasons.com/budapest ✉ V Roosevelt tér 5-6 Ⓜ M1 Vörösmarty tér 🚌 15 🚊 2, 2A

Le Meridien Budapest (5, B4)
Pest – Inner Town

Le Meridien's public areas and 218 guestrooms spread over seven floors are dripping in brocade and French polished furniture (think royalty over rock star), and many consider it the city's top five-star property.

☎ 429 5500 🖳 www.budapest.lemeridien.com ✉ V Erzsébet tér 9-10 Ⓜ M1/2/3 Deák Ferenc tér

Ask for a room with a view at the Art'otel in Víziváros

Residence Izabella (5, C2)
Pest – Andrássy út

This fabulous conversion of a 19th-century Eclectic building has 38 apartments measuring between 45 and 97 sq metres, surrounding a delightful and very tranquil central courtyard garden. The décor mixes materials such as wood, terracotta and basketry to great effect.

☎ 475 5900 🖳 www.residenceizabella.com ✉ VI Izabella utca 61 Ⓜ M1 Vörösmarty utca

TOP END

Andrássy Hotel (5, D2)
Pest – Andrássy út

This stunning five-star hotel along the main street has 70 tastefully decorated rooms (almost half of which have balconies) in a listed building. The use of etched glass and mirrors as well as wrought iron is inspired.

☎ 462 2195 🖳 www.andrassyhotel.com ✉ VI Andrássy út 111 Ⓜ M1 Hősök tere

Danubius Gellért Hotel (5, A6)
Buda – Gellért Hill

Budapest's *grande dame* is a 234-room four-star hotel with loads of character. Designed by Ármin Hegedűs in 1909 and completed in 1918, the hotel contains examples of late Art Nouveau, notably the thermal spa with its enormous arched glass entrance hall and the Zsolnay ceramic fountains in the swimming pools (free for guests). Prices depend on the room's bathroom and which way it faces.

☎ 889 5500 🖳 www.danubiusgroup.com/gellert ✉ XI Szent Gellért tér 1 🚊 18, 19, 47, 49

Danubius Grand Hotel Margitsziget (3, B3)
Margaret Island
Constructed in the late 19th century, this comfortable (rather than grand) and tranquil hotel has 164 rooms that boast all the mod cons you could want, and is connected to the Thermal Bath via a heated underground corridor, where you can take the waters for free.
☎ 889 4700 ☐ www.danubiusgroup.com/grandhotel ✉ XIII Margitsziget 🚌 26

Hotel Domina Fiesta (5, B3)
Pest – Erzsébetváros
This attractive boutique hotel, under the management of a small Italian hotel chain, has 112 tastefully furnished rooms and a vaulted wine-cellar restaurant just minutes from Pest's main square.
☎ 328 3000 ☐ www.dominahotels.it ✉ VI Király utca 20 Ⓜ M1/2/3 Deák Ferenc tér

Hotel Orion (4, C6)
Buda – the Tabán
Hidden away in the Tabán district, the Orion is a cosy place with a relaxed atmosphere and within easy walking distance of the castle. The 30 rooms are bright and of a good size.
☎ 356 8583 ☐ www.bestwestern-ce.com/orion ✉ I Döbrentei utca 13 🚋 18, 19

MIDRANGE

Büro Panzió (4, A3)
Buda – Víziváros
Just off the northern side of Moszkva tér, this *pension* looks basic from the outside, but its 10 rooms (renovated in early 2005) are comfortable and have TVs and telephones.
☎ 212 2929 ☐ http://buro-panzio.Internet tudakozo.hu ✉ II Dékán utca 3 Ⓜ M2 Moszkva tér

Carlton Hotel (4, C4)
Buda – Víziváros
A total revamp at the start of 2005 has given this 95-room hotel at the foot of Castle Hill, and at the end of a narrow cul-de-sac in Watertown (Víziváros), a cleaner, fresher look and an extra star.
☎ 224 0999 ☐ www.carltonhotel.hu ✉ I Apor Péter utca 3 🚌 86

Golden Park Hotel (5, D3)
Pest – Józsefváros
This old workhorse of a hotel has been completely de- and re-constructed, and today it is a shimmering four-star caravanserai number within spitting distance of Keleti train station. I like the bright and airy lobby, the glass doors at either end of the corridors letting in light and some of the old features they managed to retain.
☎ 477 4777 ☐ www.goldenparkhotel.com ✉ VIII Baross tér 10 Ⓜ M3 Keleti pályaudvar

Hotel Astra (4, C4)
Buda – Castle Hill
Tucked away in a small street just west of Fő utca and below the castle is this find of a hotel-cum-guesthouse, housed in a centuries-old townhouse. It has seven double rooms and three suites.
☎ 214 1906 ☐ www.hotelastra.hu ✉ I Vám utca 6 Ⓜ M2 Batthyány tér 🚌 86

Hotel Baross (5, D3)
Pest – Erzsébetváros
The flagship hotel of the Mellow Mood group of hotels and hostels (opposite), the Baross is a comfortable,

The lobby of Hotel Hold (opposite)

40-room caravanserai conveniently located directly opposite Keleti train station. The bluer-than-blue inner courtyard is a delight, and reception, which is to be found on the 5th floor, is clean and bright with a dramatic central staircase. ☎ 461 3010 ☐ www. barosshotel.hu ✉ VII Baross tér 15 Ⓜ M3 Keleti pályaudvar

Hotel Hold (5, B3)
Pest – Inner Town
The 'Moon' is an excellent choice if you want to stay in an affordable and romantic hotel right in the centre of town. The 28 rooms on two floors – there is no lift – look down onto a central covered courtyard or onto Hold utca. ☎ 472 0480 ☐ www. hotelhold.hu ✉ V Hold utca 5 Ⓜ M3 Arany János

Hotel Victoria (4, C4)
Buda – Víziváros
This hotel has 27 comfortable and spacious rooms with larger-than-life views of Parliament and the Danube. It gets special mention for its friendly service and facilities, despite its small size. The best rooms are on floors 7 to 9. ☎ 457 8080 ☐ www. victoria.hu ✉ I Bem rakpart 11 🚋 19 🚌 86

King's Hotel (5, C3)
Pest – Erzsébetváros
Budapest's only kosher hotel has 78 rooms, and is within easy walking distance of both the Orthodox and Conservative synagogues. The hotel's restaurant is *lemehadrin* (glatt) kosher and supervised by the chief rabbi of Budapest.

HOSTEL AGENCIES
As well as the hostels mentioned here, **Express** (5, B4; ☎ 327 7290, 266 3277; www.express-travel.hu; V Semmelweis utca 4) and **Mellow Mood** (5, A5; ☎ 411 2390; www.youth hostels.hu, www.mellowmood.hu; V Molnár utca 3) travel agencies are the best outfits for information about budget accommodation. Mellow Mood (affiliated with Hostelling International) runs three hostels and five budget hotels all year round, as well as six hostels that are open in summer only, mostly in Buda. It has three kiosks at Keleti train station (5, E3): **Platform 9 kiosk** (☎ 353 2722; ⏱ 7am-6pm); **Rail/bus office** (☎ 461 0948; ⏱ 6am-10pm) along platform 6; and **U Tours travel agency** (☎ 303 9818; ⏱ 7am-8pm) at the end of platform 6.

There is also **Universum** (☎ 0628 558 900; www. universumyouthhostels.hu), which has accommodation at one year-round hotel and hostel in Pest; three hostels in Buda; and a **Keleti train station booking office** (⏱ 7am–8pm) next to platform 9.

☎ 352 7675 ☐ www. kosherhotel.hu ✉ VII Nagy Diófa utca 25-27 Ⓜ M2 Blaha Lujza tér

Leó Panzió (5, B4)
Pest – Inner Town
This place would be a 'find' just on the strength of its central location, but when you factor in the low cost, this B&B is a true 'discovery'. A dozen of its 14 immaculate rooms look down on busy Kossuth Lajos utca, but they all have double-glazing and are quiet. ☎ 266 9041 ☐ www. leopanzio.hu ✉ V Kossuth Lajos utca 2/a, 2nd fl Ⓜ M3 Ferenciek tere

Marco Polo Hostel (5, C4)
Pest – Erzsébetváros
The Mellow Mood group's flagship hostel, very central and open all year round is a swish, powder-blue, 47-room place, with telephones and

TVs in all the rooms except the dorms and a lovely courtyard. Even the five spotless 12-bed dorm rooms (one reserved for women during the low season) are 'private', with beds separated by lockers and curtains. ☎ 413 2555 ☐ www. marcopolohostel.com ✉ VII Nyár utca 6 Ⓜ M2 Blaha Lujza tér

Radio Inn (5, D2)
Pest – Andrássy út
Just off leafy Andrássy út, this excellent guesthouse has 33 large one-bedroom apartments with bathroom and kitchen, 10 with two bedrooms and one with three, all spread over five floors. The lovely garden courtyard is a delight. ☎ 342 8347 ☐ www. radioinn.hu ✉ VI Benczúr utca 19 Ⓜ M1 Bajza utca

BUDGET

10 Beds (5, C3)
Pest – Erzsébetváros
OK, it's misnamed: the place has a dozen beds (in three rooms). But that's about the only thing wrong with this hostel. It's a laid-back place with a great kitchen, free use of a washing machine and an Australian owner who trusts his guests enough to give them their own set of keys. Beg, borrow and/or steal to stay here.
☎ 06 20 933 5965 💻 adrianzador@hotmail.com ✉ VII Erzsébet körút 15, 3rd fl 🚊 4, 6

Eastside Hostel (5, A2)
Pest – Szent István körút
This cosy hostel on Budapest's classy antique row is a wonderful place to stay, and readers have highly recommended it. It has three rooms with between two and six beds (not a bunk bed in sight) and free internet access. The six-bedded room has a small balcony and – wait for it – a sliver of a view of the Danube.
☎ 06 70 574 0224 💻 http://riversidebudapest.tripod.com ✉ V Falk Miksa utca 24-26, 1st fl 🚊 4, 6

Garibaldi Guesthouse (5, A3)
Pest – Inner Town
Arguably the most welcoming hostel-cum-guesthouse in Budapest, the Garibaldi has five rooms with shared bathrooms and kitchen in a flat just around the corner from Parliament. The friendly owner has at least half a dozen other apartments available in the same building.

☎ 302 3457, 06 30 951 8763 💻 garibaldiguest@hotmail.com ✉ V Garibaldi utca 5, 5th fl 🚇 M2 Kossuth Lajos tér

Green Bridge Hostel (5, B5)
Pest – Inner Town
Few hostels truly stand out in terms of comfort, location and reception, but Green Bridge has it all, in spades. Rooms from doubles to an eight-person dormitory, bunks nowhere to be seen, it's on a quiet street just one block in from the Danube and coffee is gratis throughout the day.
☎ 266 6922 💻 reservations@greenbridgehostel.com ✉ V Molnár utca 22-24 🚇 M3 Kálvin tér

Hotel Kulturinnov (4, B4)
Buda – Castle Hill
A 16-room hotel in the neo-Gothic former Finance Ministry (1904), the Kulturinnov can't be beaten for location or price on Castle Hill. The guestrooms, though clean and with private bathrooms, are not as nice as the opulent public areas of the hotel.
☎ 224 8102, 06 20 544

5396 💻 www.mka.hu ✉ I Szentháromság tér 6 🚊 16

Hotel Margitsziget (3, A5)
Margaret Island
This 11-room budget hotel in the centre of the island is surrounded by greenery and feels almost like a resort. Guests can use the tennis courts, swimming pool and sauna for free. Rooms 11 to 14 have little balconies.
☎ 329 2949 💻 www.hotelmsz.hu ✉ XIII Margitsziget 🚊 26

Red Bus Hostel (5, B4)
Pest – Inner Town
The Red Bus Hostel is a very friendly, central and well-managed place, with 28 beds in four large and airy rooms (four to five beds per room), as well as private rooms that sleep up to three people. The new branch, **Red Bus 2** (5, D3; ☎ 321 7100; VII Szövetség utca 2, 2nd fl; 🚊 73, 74, 76) has four rooms of four to five beds.
☎ 266 0136 💻 www.redbusbudapest.hu ✉ V Semmelweis utca 14, 1st fl 🚇 M2 Astoria

The Marco Polo Hostel (p73) is a good place to meet other travellers

About Budapest

HISTORY
Early Days

Around AD 100, the Romans established Aquincum (p19), as a military garrison and trading settlement; within two centuries, the Huns, a nomadic people from Asia, had pushed the Romans out. Another nomadic group, the Magyars (see below) probably reached the Carpathian Basin around the mid-9th century AD, and under the leadership of Árpád settled in present-day Hungary. Needing to form a military alliance, in 973 they appealed to the Holy Roman Emperor, and Stephen, Árpád's great-great-grandson, was crowned 'Christian King' Stephen I in 1000.

The throne passed through several European dynasties before Matthias (r 1458–90), the greatest ruler of medieval Hungary, came to power. He made Hungary one of Central Europe's leading powers, but ignored the Turkish threat, which culminated in the defeat in 1526 of Louis II (Lajos) at Mohács, a pivotal event that sent the nation into a tailspin of partition and foreign domination that lasted for centuries. Under Turkish domination, the central section of divided Hungary, including Buda, went to the Ottomans, while parts of Transdanubia went to the Austrian House of Habsburg. Turkish power began to wane in the 17th century, and with Polish assistance, Buda was liberated in 1686.

Habsburg Rule & the Dual Monarchy

With the ascension of the reformist Maria Theresa to the Habsburg throne in 1740, Hungary made great economic and cultural progress. By 1800, Pest (population 30,000) was the nation's most important commercial centre.

The wave of revolution sweeping Europe in the 19th century spurred radicalism in the city, and in 1848, after a street march demanding an end to feudalism, the government in Austria briefly allowed Hungary some autonomy, which ended when the Hungarians moved to raise a local army. The Habsburg emperor sought the assistance of the Russian tsar to defeat them, and in August 1849 martial law was declared, warfare engulfed the city and what little remained of medieval Buda and Pest was reduced to rubble.

THE MAGYARS

Magyars belong to the Finno-Ugric group of peoples, who inhabited the Ural Mountains around 4000 BC. They gradually moved southwest to Central Asia, where they lived under a tribal alliance called *onogur* (10 peoples). This is thought to be the origin of the word 'Hungary'; it has nothing to do with the tribe called the Huns. They reached the Carpathian Basin around the 9th century AD, where they met almost no resistance. Being highly skilled at riding and shooting – a common Christian prayer during the Dark Ages was 'Save us, O Lord, from the arrows of the Magyars' – they plundered and pillaged, taking slaves and amassing booty. Their raids took them as far as Spain, northern Germany and southern Italy, until they were stopped at the Battle of Augsburg by German king Otto I in 955.

Hungary was again merged into the Habsburg Empire, but the Compromise *(Ausgleich)* of 1867 created the Dual Monarchy of Austria and Hungary, and sparked a golden age in Budapest. By the turn of the 20th century, the capital's population had grown to 750,000, making it Europe's sixth-largest city.

The World Wars

In July 1914, Austria-Hungary entered WWI allied with the German empire, with disastrous results. The Habsburg monarchy was dethroned in 1918 and a republic set up in Budapest. Under the rule of right-wing 'regent' Admiral Miklós Horthy, Jews, social democrats and communists were attacked, and the lot of the working classes worsened.

In WWII, Hungary again found itself on the wrong side, and hundreds of thousands of Hungarian troops died at the Don River, covering the German retreat from Stalingrad. When Hitler learned in 1944 that Horthy was attempting to negotiate a separate peace with the Allies, the pro-Nazi Arrow Cross Party was installed in government. Jews were gathered into ghettos and, during 1944, approximately 430,000 were deported to labour camps. By the end of hostilities in April 1945, three-quarters of Budapest's homes, historical buildings and churches had been severely damaged or destroyed. As their parting gift, the Germans blew up Buda Castle and destroyed every bridge spanning the Danube.

Revolution & Reform

Limited democracy under Soviet political officers prevailed after the war, but in 1947 the communists took control and began a process of nationalisation and unfeasibly fast industrialisation. Peasants were forced into collective farms, and a network of spies and informers exposed 'class enemies' to the secret police; some were executed, many more were sent into internal exile or labour camps.

The Millenary Monument marks the conquest of the Carphathian Basin

On 23 October 1956, 50,000 university students assembled in Buda, demanding that reformist minister Imre Nagy be made prime minister. Budapest was in revolution. The next day Nagy formed a government, but after he announced that Hungary would leave the Warsaw Pact and declare itself neutral, Soviet tanks rolled in. When the fighting was over, 25,000 people were dead. Reprisals saw an estimated 20,000 people arrested and 2000 – including Nagy – executed.

After the revolt, the Hungarian Socialist Workers' Party began to liberalise the social and economic structure. By the mid-1970s, Hungary was well ahead of other Soviet-bloc countries in its standard of living and freedom of movement. But, in the 1980s, it became clear that so-called 'goulash socialism' was incapable of dealing with such problems as unemployment and soaring inflation.

In July 1989, Hungary began to demolish the electrified fence separating it from Austria. This released a wave of East Germans holidaying in Hungary into the West, and attracted thousands more. In late 1989, the communists agreed to give up their monopoly on power, paving the way for free elections in 1990. The last Soviet troops left Hungarian soil in June 1991.

> **DID YOU KNOW?**
> - Population 1.9 million
> - Unemployment around 6%
> - Inflation 3.7%
> - Average monthy wage 94,000Ft (€386) net
> - Average price of 500ml beer 400Ft

Despite initial successes curbing inflation and lowering interest rates, economic problems slowed the pace of development. In 2002, the Hungarian Socialist Party was elected, and formed a coalition government with the Alliance of Free Democrats. In April 2006, this became the first government to win consecutive general elections since 1989.

Hungary joined NATO in 1999 and, with nine other accession countries, was admitted into the EU in May 2004.

GOVERNMENT & POLITICS

Hungary's unicameral assembly sits in the Parliament building in Pest, and consists of 386 members chosen for four years. The prime minister is head of government. The head of state, the president, is elected by the house for five years.

At the most recent election in April 2006, four parties were seated in the National Assembly: the postcommunist Hungarian Socialist Party and the liberal Alliance of Free Democrats (the two coalition parties) with 210 seats, and the centre-right Alliance of Young Democrats–Hungarian Civic Party and the conservative Hungarian Democratic Forum (making up the opposition with 176 seats).

Budapest is governed by a *fővárosi önkormányzat* (municipal council), whose 66 members are elected for four-year terms, and whose leader is the city's *főpolgármester* (lord mayor).

ECONOMY

Hungary has attracted about $60 billion in foreign direct investment since 1989, the highest per-capita level in the countries of the former Eastern bloc. However, the economy grew only 4.1% in 2005, the second-slowest rate (after Poland) among the 10 states that joined the EU in 2004.

Prime Minister Ferenc Gyurcsány, reelected in April 2006, bolstered his popularity by cutting taxes, increasing child support subsidies and pensions, and trying to bring the nation's overworked roads into the 21st century. All this government spending – more than 810,000 people, or 29% of the workforce, are state employees – meant that by mid-2006 Hungary could make the dubious claim of

The impressive main dome of the Parliament building

having the largest budget deficit in Europe. A package of tax increases and austerity measures proposed by Gyurcsány to reduce the debt has eroded his popularity, as has his admission in September 2006 that the government had lied about the state of the economy to win the April election.

SOCIETY & CULTURE

The overwhelming majority of Budapest's inhabitants are Magyars (see p75) who comprise 92% of Hungary's 10 million people. Minorities include Germans (2.6%), Serbs and other South Slavs (2%), Slovaks (0.8%) and Romanians (0.7%). The number of Roma is officially put at 1.9% of the population, though some sources claim the figure is twice as high.

Throughout history, religion has often been a question of expediency here. Under King Stephen I, Catholicism won dominance over Orthodoxy and, while the majority of Hungarians were Protestant by the end of the 16th century, many changed during the Catholic Counter-Reformation under the Habsburgs. As a result, Hungarians tend to have a somewhat pragmatic approach to religion. You'll rarely see Christian churches in Budapest full, even on important holy days. The Jewish community, on the other hand, has seen a great revitalisation in recent years. Of those Hungarians declaring religious affiliation, about 52% are Roman Catholic, 16% Calvinist Protestant and nearly 3% Lutheran Protestant. Hungary's Jews number about 80,000, down from a prewar population of nearly 10 times that, with almost 90% living in Budapest.

Life expectancy is low by European standards: just over 68 years for men and almost 77 for women. The nation also has one of the highest rates of suicide (A Dubious Distinction; above right). Currently, 57% of all Hungarian marriages end in divorce.

Hungary is a highly cultured and educated society, with a literacy rate of over 99% among those aged 15 and over. In general, Hungarians are not uninhibited like the extrovert Romanians or sentimental Slavs. They are reserved, somewhat formal people – forget the impassioned, devil-may-care, Gypsy-fiddling stereotype. The national anthem calls Hungarians 'a people torn by fate', and the overall mood is one of *honfibú* (literally 'patriotic sorrow'), which predates what they call *az átkos 40 év* (the accursed 40 years) of communism.

> ## A DUBIOUS DISTINCTION
> Hungary has one of the world's highest suicide rates – 60.1 per 100,000 people in 2001, surpassed only by Russia and several other former Soviet republics. Some say that Hungarians' inclination to gloom leads to an ultimate act of despair. Others link it to a phenomenon not uncommon here in the late 19th century. As the aristocracy withered away, the *kisnemesség* (minor nobility) would do themselves in to 'save their name and honour'. As a result, suicide was – and is – not looked upon dishonourably as such, and victims may be buried in hallowed ground. About 60% of suicides are by hanging.

Hungarians let their hair down in warm weather, and you'll see plenty of public displays of affection. It's all very romantic, but beware: in the remoter corners of Budapest's parks, and on Margaret Island, you may stumble upon more passionate displays.

Etiquette

Hungarians are extremely polite, and the language can be very courtly – even when doing business with the butcher or having your hair cut. The standard greeting for a man to a woman (or youngsters to their elders, regardless of gender) is *Csókolom* ('I kiss it' – 'it' being the hand). People of all ages – even close friends – shake hands profusely when meeting up.

Clinking glasses when drinking beer is a no-no, as it's believed that's what the Habsburgs did after executing the revolutionaries of 1849 (see p75).

If you are invited to a Hungarian home, bring a bunch of flowers or a bottle of good local wine (see p41). You can talk about anything under the sun – from religion and politics to whether the Hungarian language really is more difficult than Japanese – but traditionally, the discussion of money is considered to be gauche in Hungary. Do not expect (or ask for) a tour of the house or apartment; that is just not done here.

ARTS
Music & Dance

Franz – or Ferenc – Liszt (1811–86), Hungary's greatest composer, established the Academy of Music in Budapest. He described himself

Art Nouveau mosaics are a common feature of Budapest

as 'part Gypsy', and some of his works, notably the 20 *Hungarian Rhapsodies,* echo the traditional music of the Roma.

Ferenc Erkel (1810–93), the first musical director of the Hungarian State Opera House, is the father of Magyar opera. Two of his works – the stirringly nationalistic *Bánk Bán* and *László Hunyadi* – are staples of the opera house. Erkel also composed the music for the Hungarian national anthem, *Himnusz.*

Béla Bartók (1881–1945) and Zoltán Kodály (1882–1967) made the first systematic study of Hungarian folk music. Both integrated their findings into their own compositions – Bartók in *Bluebeard's Castle,* and Kodály in his *Peacock Variations.*

It is important to distinguish between 'Gypsy' music and Hungarian folk music. Gypsy music as it is known and heard in Hungarian restaurants from Budapest to Boston is urban schmaltz based on old recruiting tunes called *verbunkos*. At least two fiddles, a bass and a cymbalom (a curious stringed instrument played with sticks) are *de rigueur*. For more on Hungarian folk, see p65.

Real Roma – as opposed to Gypsy – music traditionally does not use instruments but is sung a cappella (though sometimes it is backed with percussion and even guitar). Two of the best-known modern Roma groups are Kalyi Jag (Black Fire) and Romano Drom.

Architecture

The Mongols, Turks and Habsburgs destroyed most of Budapest's Romanesque and Gothic architecture, but the Royal Palace (p8) incorporates many Gothic features, and the *sedilia* (niches with seats) on Castle Hill (p31) are pure Gothic. The chapels in the Inner Town Parish Church (p24) have some fine Gothic and Renaissance tabernacles, and you can't miss the Renaissance stonework at the Hungarian National Gallery (p22).

Baroque architecture abounds here. The Citadella (p27) on Gellért Hill and the municipal council office (p32) in Pest are baroque in its civic or secular form.

Art Nouveau architecture (and its Viennese variant, Secessionism) is Budapest's signature style; (see p26). Art Nouveau flourished in Europe and the USA from about 1890 to 1910. Fortunately, prewar economic and political torpor, and the 40-year 'big sleep' after WWII, left many Art Nouveau buildings here beaten but standing – many more, in fact, than remain in such important Art Nouveau 'centres' as Paris, Brussels and Vienna. In Budapest, the use of traditional façades with allegorical and historical figures and scenes, folk motifs and Zsolnay ceramics and other local materials led to an Eclectic style. Its master was Ödön Lechner (1845–1914), and his most ambitious works are the Applied Arts Museum (p20) and the Royal Postal Savings Bank (p27).

Painting & Sculpture

Distinctly Hungarian art didn't come into its own until the mid-19th century. The romantic nationalist school of heroic paintings, best exemplified by Bertalan Székely (1835–1910), who painted much of the interior of Matthias Church (p8), gave way to the realism of Mihály Munkácsy (1844–1900). But the greatest painters from this period were Kosztka Tivadar Csontváry (1853–1919) and József Rippl-Rónai (1861–1927), whose works are on display at the Hungarian National Gallery (p22).

The 20th-century painter Viktor Vasarely (1908–97), the so-called 'father of op art', has his own museum (p23), as does the contemporary sculptor Imre Varga (p22). A turning point for modern art in Hungary came in 2005 when the Ludwig Museum of Contemporary Art (p22) moved from Castle Hill to its new, purpose-built premises in the Palace of Arts.

Literature

Sándor Petőfi (1823–49) is Hungary's most celebrated poet. A line from his *National Song* became the rallying cry for the 1848–49 War of Independence, in which Petőfi fought and died. A deeply philosophical play called *The Tragedy of Man* by his colleague, Imre Madách (1823–64), is still considered to be the country's greatest classical drama.

Zsigmond Móricz (1879–1942), one of the cofounders of the influential literary magazine *Nyugat* (*West*; 1908), examined the harshness of peasant life in the tradition of the French naturalist Émile Zola. Socialist poet Attila József (1905–37), raised in the slums of Ferencváros, expressed the alienation felt by individuals in the modern age; his poem *By the Danube* is brilliant even in translation.

In 2002, novelist and Auschwitz survivor Imre Kertész (1929–) became the first Hungarian to be awarded the Nobel Prize for Literature. For other recommended books by Hungarian authors see p44.

Cinema

The scarcity of government grants has limited the production of quality Hungarian films in recent years, but a handful of good (and even great) ones still get produced. For classics, look out for anything by Oscar-winning István Szabó *(Sweet Emma, Dear Böbe, The Taste of Sunshine)*, Miklós Jancsó *(Outlaws)* and Péter Bacsó *(The Witness, Live Show)*. Other favourites are *Simon Mágus,* the surrealistic tale of two magicians and a young woman in Paris directed by Ildikó Enyedi, and her more recent *Tender Interface,* which deals with the brain-drain from Hungary after WWII. For our list of films that use Budapest as a backdrop, see p68.

Directory

ARRIVAL & DEPARTURE
Air
Ferihegy International Airport (1, off C3; ☎ 296 7000; www.bud.hu) is 24km southeast of the city centre.

AIRPORT ACCESS
Minibus
The Airport Minibus Service (☎ 296 8555; single/return 2300/3900Ft) ferries passengers from Ferihegy directly to their accommodation; tickets available in the arrival halls.

Taxi
Call one of the companies listed on p84; and expect to pay about 5000Ft. If you book in advance, Tele 5 (☎ 355 5555) charges 3490Ft from the airport to Pest, and 3990Ft to Buda.

Bus
The cheapest, but most time-consuming way to get into town is to take the airport bus (look for the stop marked 'BKV Plusz Reptér busz' between Terminals 2A and 2B), terminating at Kőbánya-Kispest metro station. From there, take the M3 metro into the centre. The total cost is 320Ft.

CLIMATE CHANGE & TRAVEL

Travel – especially air travel – is a significant contributor to global climate change. At Lonely Planet, we believe that all travellers have a responsibility to limit their personal impact. As a result, we have teamed up with Rough Guides and other concerned industry partners to support Climatecare.org, which allows travellers to offset the greenhouse gases they are responsible for with contributions to sustainable travel schemes. Lonely Planet offsets all staff and author travel. For more information, check out www.lonelyplanet.com.

Bus
Eurolines (☎ 219 8021; www.eurolines.com), linking Budapest with points abroad from Bratislava to London, and its Hungarian associate **Volánbusz** (☎ 382 0888; www.volanbusz.hu) have offices at Népliget bus station.

Népliget bus station (2, B3; ☎ 219 8000; IX Üllői út 131) International (and some domestic) buses

Stadionok bus station (2, B2; ☎ 251 0125; XIV Hungária körút 48-52) Buses to cities and towns east of Budapest

Etele tér bus station (2, A3; ☎ 382 4900; XI Etele tér) Buses to southwest Hungary

Árpád Bridge bus station (2, A1; ☎ 329 1450; XIII Róbert Károly körút) Buses to the Danube Bend and northern Hungary

Széna tér bus station (4, A3; ☎ 201 3688; I Széna tér 1/a) Buses to towns northwest of Budapest

Train
Magyar Államvasutak (Hungarian State Railways, MÁV; ticket office; 5, C2; ☎ 461 5500, 352 2800; VI Andrássy út 35) links up with the European rail network in all directions; for fares, check www.elvira.hu.

Keleti train station (5, E3; ☎ 313 6835; VIII Kerepesi út 2-6) Most international trains

Nyugati train station (5, B2; ☎ 349 0115; VI Teréz körút 55-57) Trains to certain destinations in the east (eg Romania)

Déli train station (4, A4; ☎ 375 6293, 355 8657; I Krisztina körút 37) Trains to some destinations in the south (eg Osijek in Croatia, and Sarajevo in Bosnia)

INFORMATION
24-hour information on international train services ☎ 461 5500, 06 40 494 949

MÁV international information & ticket centre (☎ 461 5500, 352 2800; VI Andrássy út 35)

Boat

Mahart PassNave (5, B5; ☎ 484 4013; www.mahartpassnave.hu; V Belgrád rakpart) runs a hydrofoil service between Budapest and Vienna (5½ to 6½ hours, single/return €79/99) daily from early April to October (passengers may disembark at Bratislava with advance notice). Ferries arrive and depart from the **International Ferry Pier** (Nemzetközi hajóállomás; 5, B5; V Belgrád rakpart), between Elizabeth and Liberty Bridges on the Pest side.

Customs & Duty Free

The usual allowances apply to duty-free goods purchased outside the EU, eg 200 cigarettes, 50 cigars or 250g of loose tobacco; 2L of still wine; and 1L of spirits. You must declare the import/export of any amount of cash, cheques, securities etc exceeding 1 million Ft. When leaving the country, you cannot take out valuable antiques without a permit; see p42 for more details.

Left Luggage

There is a 24-hour left-luggage service in Terminal B of the **airport** (per item per 1/3/6hr 350/1050/1400Ft, per day/week 2200/6500Ft), and at **Népliget** (per piece per day 190Ft; ☺ 6am-9pm) and **Stadionok** (per piece 200Ft; ☺ 6am-7pm) bus stations.

GETTING AROUND

Budapest has an ageing but safe, efficient and inexpensive public transport system run by **BKV** (www.bkv.hu). The *Budapesti Közlekedési Hálózata Térképe* (Budapest Transport Network Map; 380Ft) is available at most metro ticket counters. Services run from about 4am to between 9pm and 11.30pm. From 11.30pm to 4am, some 30 night buses (always with three digits and beginning with '9') operate every 10 to 60 minutes.

The basic fare is 185Ft (1665/3145Ft for a block of 10/20 tickets), allowing you to travel as far as you like on the same vehicle. You can buy tickets at kiosks, newsstands or metro entrances, and they have to be validated in machines at metro entrances and aboard other vehicles. Travelling without a valid ticket is risky; there's an excellent chance you'll get caught. However, conductors are now authorised to issue tickets, rather than fines, to foreign tourists without tickets.

Travel Passes

Passes are valid on all trams, buses, trolleybuses, HÉV trains (within city limits) and metro lines. A one-day pass is poor value at 1150Ft, but the three-day pass known as the *touristajegy* (tourist ticket) for 2500Ft, and the seven-day pass known as the *hetijegy* (weekly ticket) for 3400Ft, are worthwhile.

Metro & HÉV

Budapest has three underground metro lines that converge at V Deák Ferenc tér: the yellow M1 line from Vörösmarty tér to Mexikói út in Pest; the red M2 line from Déli train station in Buda to Örs vezér tere in Pest; and the blue M3 line from Újpest-Központ to Kőbánya-Kispest in Pest. It also has the HÉV, an above-ground commuter train line.

Tram

The most important tram lines are:

2 & 2A – Scenic trams along the Pest side of the Danube

4 & 6 – XI Fehérvári út and XI Móricz Zsigmond körtér in south Buda respectively, following the entire length of the 'Big Ring Road' in Pest and terminating at II Moszkva tér in Buda

18 – Southern Buda along XI Bartók Béla út through the Tabán to II Moszkva tér

47 & 49 – V Deák Ferenc tér in Pest to southern Buda via the 'Little Ring Road'

Bus

Some buses you might find useful are:

4 – Northern Pest via VI Hősök tere to
V Deák Ferenc tér

105 – V Deák Ferenc tér to XII Apor Vilmos
tér in central Buda

Night bus 906 – Follows tram 6's route
along the Big Ring Road

Night bus 907 – M2 Örs vezér tere metro
stop in Pest to Kelenföld station in Buda

Várbusz – a minibus with a logo of a
castle, labelled 'Várbusz' and costing one
metro ticket, links the M2 metro at
II Moszkva tér with I Dísz tér on Castle Hill
via I Várfok utca

Trolleybus

Useful trolleybuses are the ones to and
around the City Park (70, 72 and 74) and
Népliget (75 and 77).

Taxi

I've heard from many readers who were
grossly overcharged and even threatened
by taxi drivers. Never get into a cab that
does not have a yellow licence plate and
an identification badge displayed on the
dashboard, the logo of one of the reputable
taxi firms listed here on the side doors and a
table of fares posted prominently.

From 6am to 10pm, the highest flag-
down fee that can be legally charged is
300Ft, the per-kilometre charge 240Ft and
the waiting fee 60Ft. Fees after 10pm are
420/330/80Ft.

Buda ☎ 233 3333
City ☎ 211 1111
Fő ☎ 222 2222

Boat

Between May and mid-September, passenger
ferries run by **BKV** (☎ 369 1359; www.bkv.
hu) depart from IX Boráros tér (5, C6) beside
Petőfi Bridge between six and eight times
daily, and head for Óbuda, a two-hour trip
with 10 stops. Tickets (adult/child 600/300Ft
from end to end) are sold on board.

Car

Driving in Budapest can be a nightmare:
ongoing roadworks reduce traffic to a snail's
pace, and parking spots are difficult to
find. If you need to drive, all the international car-rental firms have offices in
Budapest.

Anselport (☎ 362 6080, 06 20 945 0279;
www.anselport.hu; XXII V utca 22)

Fox Autorent (☎ 382 9000; www.fox-
autorent.com; XXII Nagytétényi út 48-50)

PRACTICALITIES
Business Hours

Nyitva means 'open', *zárva* is 'closed'. The
following hours are only a guide; hours may
fluctuate depending on location and time
of year.

Shops & businesses 10am-6pm Mon-Fri,
10am-1pm Sat

Banks 7.45am-5pm or -6pm Mon, 7.45am-
4pm or -5pm Tue-Thu, 7.45am-4pm Fri

Post offices Main offices: 8am-7pm or
-8pm Mon-Fri, 8am-noon Sat; branch
offices: 8am-4pm Mon-Fri

Restaurants 10am or 11am-11pm or
midnight

Climate

January is the coldest month (with the
temperature averaging −4°C), and July and
August the hottest (average temperature
26°C during each). Spring arrives in early
April, and is often quite wet. Summer can
be very hot and dry. It rains for most of
November, and doesn't usually get cold
until mid-December. Winter is relatively
short, often cloudy and damp, but

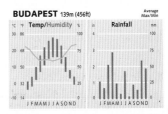

BUDAPEST 139m (456ft)

sometimes brilliantly sunny. What little snow the city gets usually disappears after a few days.

Disabled Travellers

Budapest has made great strides in recent years in making public areas and facilities more accessible to the disabled. Wheelchair ramps, toilets fitted for the disabled and audible traffic signals for the blind, though not as common as they are in Western Europe, do exist.

INFORMATION & ORGANISATIONS
Hungarian Federation of Disabled Persons' Associations (☎ 250 9013, 388 2387; www.meoszinfo.hu)

Discounts
Budapest Card (☎ 266 0479; www.budapestinfo.hu; 48/72hr 5200/6500Ft) Free or reduced admission to 60 museums and sights, unlimited travel on public transport and other discounts; available from Tourinform offices, travel agencies, hotels and main metro stations

Electricity
The electric current in Budapest is 220V, 50Hz AC. Plugs are the European type with two round pins.

Embassies
Australia (4, off A5; ☎ 457 9777; XII Királyhágó tér 8-9, 4th fl)
Canada (4, B2; ☎ 392 3360; II Ganz utca 12-14)
Germany (4, B4; ☎ 488 3505; I Úri utca 64-66)
UK (5, A4; ☎ 266 2888; V Harmincad utca 6)
USA (5, B3; ☎ 475 4164; V Szabadság tér 12)

Emergency & Safety
No parts of Budapest are off-limits, although some locals avoid Margaret Island after dark off-season, and the dodgier parts of the 8th and 9th districts (prostitution areas). Pickpocketing is most common in markets, Váci utca and Hősök tere, on Castle Hill, near major hotels and on certain popular buses (eg 7) and trams (2, 2A, 4, 6, 47 and 49).

Scams that involve attractive young women, gullible guys, expensive nightclub drinks and forced ATM visits have been common for a decade; I still get letters from male readers complaining they've been ripped off.

Ambulance ☎ 104
Central emergency number (English spoken) ☎ 112
English-language crime hotline (8am-8pm) ☎ 438 8080 (8pm-8am) ☎ 0680 660 044
Fire ☎ 105, 321 6216
Police ☎ 107

Fitness
SWIMMING
The pools attached to the Gellért, Lukács, Széchenyi and Rudas thermal baths (p10) are recommended.
Alfréd Hajós National Sports Pool (3, A5; ☎ 450 4214, 340 4946; XIII Margitsziget) One indoor and three outdoor pools, where Olympic swimming and water-polo teams train
Dagály Pools (3, C2; ☎ 452 4500; XIII Népfürdő utca 36) Huge complex with a total of 10 pools, plenty of grass and shade

HEALTH CLUBS
A daily ticket into the thermal bath and pools at the Danubius Grand Hotel Margitsziget (p72) includes use of the fitness room and machines.
Astoria Fitness Centre (5, C4; ☎ 343 1140; V Dohány utca 32)
A&TSA Fitness Club (4, A5; ☎ 488 7220; I Pálya utca 9)

Gay & Lesbian Travellers

The gay and (less so) lesbian communities are quite active in Budapest, but keep a relatively low profile. For entertainment listings, see p64. The free pamphlet *Na Végre!* (*At Last!*; navegre@hotmail.com) has information on venues, events and parties. Useful websites are www.budapestgayvisitor.hu and http://budapest.gayguide.net.

Háttér Gay & Lesbian Association
(☎ 329 3380, 06 40 200 358; www.hatter.hu) Advice and helpline

Budapest Gayguide.net (☎ 06 30 932 3334; http://budapestgayguide.net) Advice and information

Health

Foreigners are entitled to first-aid and ambulance services only when they have suffered an accident and require immediate medical attention; follow-up treatment and medicine must be paid for. EU citizens on public-health insurance schemes are generally covered by reciprocal arrangements in Hungary. They should, however, carry their European Health Insurance Card. In the UK, application forms are available from the Department of Health (www.dh.gov.uk).

MEDICAL SERVICES

FirstMed Centers (4, B3; ☎ 224 9090; www.firstmedcenters.com; I Hattyú utca 14, 5th fl; ☯ 24hr emergency) Basic consultation 12,600/25,200Ft for up to 10/20 minutes

DENTAL SERVICES

SOS Dental Service (5, B3; ☎ 267 9602, 269 6010; VI Király utca 14; ☯ 24hr) Consultation 2000Ft, extractions 5000Ft to 6000Ft, fillings 6000Ft to 10,000Ft

PHARMACIES

Csillag Gyógyszertár (5, C4; ☎ 314 3695; VIII Rákóczi út 39; ☯ 7.30am-9pm Mon-Fri, 7.30am-2pm Sat)

Déli Gyógyszertár (4, A4; ☎ 355 4691; XII Alkotás utca 1/b; ☯ 8am-8pm Mon-Fri, 8am-2pm Sat)

Holidays

New Year's Day 1 January
1848 Revolution Day 15 March
Easter Monday March/April
May Day 1 May
Whit Monday May/June
St Stephen's Day 20 August
1956 Remembrance Day 23 October
All Saints' Day 1 November
Christmas holidays 25-26 December

Internet Access

Blue signs announcing 'eMagyarország Pont' tell you that you can log on nearby. Many libraries have free terminals; elsewhere access is from 200 to 600Ft per hour.

INTERNET CAFÉS

CEU NetPoint (5, A3; ☎ 328 3506; www.ceunet.ceu.hu; V Október 6 utca 14)
Electric Café (5, C4; ☎ 413 1803; www.electriccafé.hu; VII Dohány utca 37)
Nagyi Palacsintázója (4, B3;
☎ 418 0721; V Petőfi Sándor tér 17-19;
☯ 24hr)
Parknet (5, B4; ☎ 270 2249; V Váci utca 23)
Private Link (5, C5; ☎ 334 2057; www.private-link.hu; VIII József körút 52;
☯ 24hr)

INTERNET RESOURCES

LonelyPlanet.com (www.lonelyplanet.com) An excellent resource with Budapest accommodation reviews and online booking
Budapest Week Online (www.budapestweek.com) Especially good for arts and entertainment
MTI (www.mti.hu) Government-funded news agency, with up-to-date news and opinions

Budapest Sun Online (www. budapestsun.com) Local news, interviews and features

Visitors' Guide Budapest (www. visitorsguide.hu) The *Budapest Sun*'s guide

Pestiside (www.pestiside.hu) My favourite Budapest website; useful in all respects

Lost Property

If you've left something on public transport, contact the **BKV Lost & Found Office** (5, C3; ☎ 267 5299; VII Akácfa utca 18; ⏱ 8am-5pm Mon, Tue, Thu & Fri, 8am-6pm Wed).

Metric System

Hungary uses the metric system for weights and measures.

TEMPERATURE

$$°C = (°F - 32) \div 1.8$$
$$°F = (°C \times 1.8) + 32$$

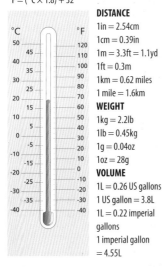

DISTANCE

1in = 2.54cm
1cm = 0.39in
1m = 3.3ft = 1.1yd
1ft = 0.3m
1km = 0.62 miles
1 mile = 1.6km

WEIGHT

1kg = 2.2lb
1lb = 0.45kg
1g = 0.04oz
1oz = 28g

VOLUME

1L = 0.26 US gallons
1 US gallon = 3.8L
1L = 0.22 imperial gallons
1 imperial gallon = 4.55L

Money
CURRENCY

Hungary's currency is the forint (Ft). There are coins of 1Ft, 2Ft, 5Ft, 10Ft, 20Ft, 50Ft and 100Ft. Notes come in 200Ft, 500Ft, 1000Ft, 2000Ft, 5000Ft, 10,000Ft and 20,000Ft.

ATMS

There are automated teller machines everywhere in Budapest, including train and bus stations, and quite a few foreign-currency exchange machines.

CHANGING MONEY

Avoid moneychangers (especially those on V Váci utca) in favour of banks. Be sure to arrive about an hour before closing to ensure the *bureau de change* counter is still open.

K&H (5, B5; V Váci utca 40; ⏱ 8am-5pm Mon, 8am-4pm Tue-Thu, 8am-3pm Fri; Ⓜ M3 Ferenciek tere)

CREDIT CARDS

Visa, MasterCard and American Express are widely accepted, and you'll be able to use them at many restaurants, shops, hotels and travel agencies.

Newspapers & Magazines

Two English-language weekly newspapers are available: the tabloid *Budapest Sun* (399Ft; Thursdays), with a useful arts and entertainment supplement; and the *Budapest Times* (420Ft; Mondays), with good reviews and opinion pieces. The erudite *Hungarian Quarterly* (1500Ft) looks at issues in great depth, and is a valuable source of current Hungarian thinking.

The best place for foreign-language newspapers and magazines is **Világsajtó Háza** (World Press House; 5, B4; ☎ 317 1311; V Városház utca 3-5). Almost as good is **Immedio** (5, A4; ☎ 318 5604; V Váci utca 10).

Post

The Hungarian Postal Service (Magyar Posta; www.posta.hu) has improved greatly in recent years, but post offices are usually still crowded, service is slow and staff generally speak Hungarian only. To beat the crowds, ask at kiosks, newsagents or stationery shops if they sell stamps *(bélyeg)*. The **main post office** (5, B4; V Petőfi Sándor utca 13-15) is a few minutes' walk from Deák Ferenc tér.

POSTAL RATES

Sending letters within Hungary costs 52Ft (90Ft priority), for the rest of Europe 170Ft (190Ft priority). Airmail *(légiposta)* letters of up to 20/50g are 185/270Ft within Europe, and 210/350Ft for the rest of the world. Postcards cost 52Ft to send within Hungary, 120Ft within the rest of Europe and 140Ft to the rest of the world.

Radio

The public Magyar Rádió has three stations, named after Lajos Kossuth (jazz and news; 98.6AM), Sándor Petőfi (1960s to 1980s music, news and sport; 94.8FM) and Béla Bartók (classical music and news; 105.3FM). Radio Budapest (www.english. radio.hu) broadcasts in English on 88.1FM and 91.9FM. Juventus (89.5FM) is a popular music station, Rádió 88 (95.4FM) plays the top music of the 1980s and 1990s, and Danubius Rádió (98.3 and 103.3FM) is a mix of popular music and news.

Telephone

You can make domestic and international calls from public telephones, which are usually in good working order. They work with both coins and phonecards; the latter are now far more common.

All localities in Hungary have a two-digit telephone area code, except for Budapest, which has one digit (☎ 1). To make a local call, pick up the receiver and listen for the continuous dial tone, then dial the number. For an intercity landline call within Hungary, and whenever you are calling a mobile phone, dial ☎ 06 and wait for the second, more melodious, tone. To call Budapest from overseas, dial ☎ + 36 1.

PHONECARDS

There are many phonecards on offer, such as T-Com's **Barangoló** (☎ 0680 501 255; www.magyartelekom.hu) in denominations of 400Ft, 1000Ft, 2000Ft and 5000Ft, and **NeoPhone** (☎ 0680 188 202; www.neophone.hu) cards valued at 300Ft, 1000Ft, 2000Ft and 5000Ft. Sample per-minute costs are 25Ft to most European countries and the USA, and 29Ft to Australia and New Zealand.

MOBILE PHONES

Buying a rechargeable SIM card will reduce the cost of making local calls (between 19Ft and 27Ft a minute) to a fraction of what you'd pay using your home SIM. For example, **Vodafone** (5, B2; ☎ 238 7281, 238 7588; Shop 46, 4th fl, West End City Centre, VI Váci út 3) has prepaid vouchers available for 1000/2500Ft with 500/1500Ft worth of credit.

USEFUL PHONE NUMBERS

Directory enquiries ☎ 198
International access code ☎ 00
International operator ☎ 199
Country code ☎ 36

Television

Magyar Televízió controls two channels, M1 and M2. There is a public satellite channel. Duna TV and there are two main private channels, TV2 and RTL Klub, some 20 private cable and satellite channels nationwide, broadcasting everything from game and talk shows to classic Hungarian films. Most midrange and top-end hotels and *pensions* in Budapest have satellite TV, mainly in German.

Time

Winter time is GMT plus one hour; summer time is GMT plus two hours. Clocks are advanced at 2am on the last Sunday in March, and set back at the same time on the last Sunday in October.

Tipping

Nearly everyone in Budapest will routinely tip waiters, hairdressers and taxi drivers. Doctors and dentists accept 'gratitude money', and even petrol-station and thermal-spa attendants expect something. If you aren't impressed with the service, leave little or nothing at all. To learn more about the unusual way to tip a waiter, see p47.

Tourist Information
TOURIST OFFICES

Budapest Tourist Office (☎ 266 0479; www.buda pestinfo.hu) Three outlets: Castle Hill branch (4, B4; ☎ 488 0475; I Szentháromság tér; ☺ 9am-8pm May-Sep, 10am-7pm Oct-Apr); Oktogon branch (5, C3; ☎ 322 4098; VI Liszt Ferenc tér 11; ☺ 9am-7pm Apr-Oct, 10am-6pm Nov-Mar); and Nyugati train station branch (5, B2; ☎ 302 8580; Nyugati pályaudvar, platform 10; ☺ 9am-7pm Apr-Oct,9am-6pm Nov-Mar; also offices at Ferihegy airport's Terminals 1, 2A (arrivals) and 2B (departures)

Tourinform (5, B4; ☎ 438 8080, ☎ 24hr information hotline 06-80 630 800; www. tourinform.hu; V Sütő utca 2; ☺ 8am-8pm) Usually the best source of information but can get hopelessly crowded in summer; staff sometimes unhelpful

Women Travellers

Hungarian men can be sexist in their thinking, but women in Budapest do not suffer any particular form of harassment. If you do need assistance and/or information, ring the **Women's Line** (Nővonal; ☎ 0680 505 101; ☺ 6-10pm Thu-Tue) or **Women for Women against Violence** (NANE; ☎ 267 4900; info@nane.hu).

LANGUAGE

Hungarians like to boast that their language ranks with Japanese and Arabic as among the world's most difficult tongues to learn.

It is true, but you shouldn't let that put you off attempting a few words and phrases. For assorted reasons – the compulsory study of Russian in all schools until the late 1980s being one of them – Hungarians are not polyglots and even when they do have a smattering of a foreign language, they lack experience and are generally hesitant to speak it. Attempt a few words in *magyarul* (Hungarian), and they will be impressed, take it as a compliment and be extremely encouraging.

Pronunciation
VOWELS

a	as in 'hot'
á	as in 'father'
e	as in 'bet'
é	as in 'air'
i	as in 'hit'
í	as in 'meet'
o	as in 'law' but short
ó	as in 'awl'
ö	as in 'curt' but short (with no 'r' sound)
ő	as in 'her' (with no 'r' sound)
u	as in 'pull'
ú	as in 'rule'
ü	like i but with rounded lips (like 'u' in French *tu*)
ű	as in 'strewn'

CONSONANTS

c	as the 'ts' in 'rats'
cs	as the 'ch' in 'cheese'
dz	as in 'adze'
dzs	as the 'j' in 'joke'
gy	as the 'du' in 'dune' (British)
j/ly	as in 'yes'
ny	as the 'ny' in 'canyon'
r	as in 'run' (but rolled)
s	as the 'sh' in 'ship'
sz	as the 's' in 'sit'
ty	as the 'tu' in 'tube' (British)
zs	as the 's' in 'pleasure'

USEFUL WORDS AND PHRASES

Hello.	*Szervusz. (singular)*
	Szervusztok. (plural)
Hi.	*Szia/Sziasztok. (sg/pl)*
Good ...	*Jó ... kívánok.*
morning	*reggelt*
afternoon/day	*napot*
evening	*estét*
Goodbye.	*Viszlát. (polite)*
	Szia. (informal sg)
	Sziasztok. (inf sg/pl)
Good night.	*Jó éjszakát.*
Yes.	*Igen.*
No.	*Nem.*
Please.	*Kérem. (pol)*
	Kérlek. (inf)
Thank you (very much).	*(Nagyon) Köszönöm.*
You're welcome.	*Szívesen.*
Excuse me.	*Elnézést kérek.*
Sorry.	*Sajnálom.*
How are you?	*Hogy van? (pol)*
	Hogy vagy? (inf)
Fine.	*Jól.*
What's your name?	*Mi a neve? (pol)*
	Mi a neved? (inf)
My name is ...	*A nevem ...*
Do you speak English?	*Beszél angolul?*
I (don't) understand.	*(Nem) Értem.*

Numbers

0	*nulla*
1	*egy*
2	*kettő*
3	*három*
4	*négy*
5	*öt*
6	*hat*
7	*hét*
8	*nyolc*
9	*kilenc*
10	*tíz*
50	*ötven*
100	*száz*
1000	*ezer*

Days

Monday	*hétfő*
Tuesday	*kedd*
Wednesday	*szerda*
Thursday	*csütörtök*
Friday	*péntek*
Saturday	*szombat*
Sunday	*vasárnap*

Emergencies

Help!	*Segítség!*
Could you please help?	*Tudna segíteni?*
Call the police!	*Hívja a rendőrséget!*
Call a doctor!	*Hívjon orvost!*
Where's the police station?	*Hol a rendőrség?*
Go away!	*Menjen el!*

Signs

Bejárat	Entrance
Kijárat	Exit
Nyitva	Open
Zárva	Closed
Foglalt	Reserved/Occupied
Belépni Tilos	No Entry
Tilos	Prohibited
Tilos a Dohányzás	No Smoking
Toalett/WC	Toilets
Férfiak	Men
Nők	Women

Index

See also separate indexes for Eating (p93), Shopping (p93), Sights with map references (p93) and Sleeping (p94).

EATING

SHOPPING

SIGHTS INDEX

SLEEPING

Map Legend

FEATURES

🍴	Károlyi Étterem	*Eating*
🎵	Fat Mo's Music Club	*Entertainment*
🍷	Darshan Udvar	*Drinking*
☕	Gerbeaud	*Café*
🕍	Great Synagogue	*Highlights*
🛍	Porcelánház	*Shopping*
🏛	Citadella	*Sights/Activities*
🏨	Hotel Orion	*Sleeping*
●	Szentendre	*Trips & Tours*

AREAS

	Beach, Desert
	Building
	Land
	Mall
	Other Area
	Park/Cemetery
	Sports
	Urban

HYDROGRAPHY

	River, Creek
	Intermittent River
	Swamp
	Water

BOUNDARIES

	State, Provincial
	Regional, Suburb
	Ancient Wall

ROUTES

	Tollway
	Freeway
	Primary Road
	Secondary Road
	Tertiary Road
	Lane
	Under Construction
	One-Way Street
	Unsealed Road
	Mall/Steps
	Tunnel
	Walking Path
	Walking Trail/Track
	Pedestrian Overpass
	Walking Tour

TRANSPORT

	Airport, Airfield
	Bus Route
	Cycling, Bicycle Path
	Ferry
	General Transport
	Metro
	Monorail
	Rail
	Taxi Rank
	Tram

SYMBOLS

🏦	Bank, ATM	🕎	Jewish
🔴	Buddhist	🔦	Lighthouse
🏰	Castle, Fortress	👁	Lookout
🔵	Christian	🗿	Monument
🤿	Diving, Snorkeling	▲	Mountain, Volcano
🔵	Embassy, Consulate	🏞	National Park
⊕	Hospital, Clinic	🅿	Parking Area
❶	Information	⛽	Petrol Station
@	Internet Access	📷	Picnic Area
☪	Islamic	●	Point of Interest
		⊛	Police Station
		🏣	Post Office
		🔵	Ruin
		☎	Telephone
		🚻	Toilets
		🌊	Waterfall
		🐦	Zoo, Bird Sanctuary